The Executive Entrepreneur

Jim Stovall and Paula Marshall

Published by Expert Message Group, LLC

Expert Message Group, LLC
P.O. Box 949
Tulsa, OK 74101

415.523.0404

www.expertmessagegroup.com

First Printing, 2012

ISBN 978-1-936875-08-5

Printed in the United States of America

Set in Garamond 11/16

For permissions, please contact:

Expert Message Group, LLC
P.O. Box 949
Tulsa, OK 74101

Contents

Introduction

I have advised many startups and midlevel companies over the years, and have noticed one major problem in the business world: as a general rule, entrepreneurs can't manage, and managers can't be entrepreneurial. On the rare occasions when I have come into contact with an individual who possessed both skill sets, it was apparent that that person was headed for greatness.

Let me explain what I mean a little better. An entrepreneur must be creative, dynamic and constantly on the lookout for new opportunities. An executive must be stable, judicious and able to maintain the status quo. By their very natures, the entrepreneur and the executive are at odds with each other. However, I have found in my career that I have needed to hone both sides of myself in order to be successful. Over the course of a company's life cycle, the skills of either an entrepreneur or an executive will be called upon, and many times the leader of that company will find him or herself oscillating between both roles up to hundreds of times in a day.

The bottom line for companies that aren't growing is that their executives aren't being entrepreneurial, and entrepreneurs that don't survive end up losing everything because they never learned how to be an executive. The purpose of this book is to help bridge the gap.

As you'll read in the pages ahead, I founded my company, Narrative Television Network, on little more than a dream in the basement of an apartment building. Today we have an Emmy award, and we do work with 20th Century

Fox, NBC, ABC and many of the other large entertainment networks that you interact with every day. For much of my career, I was the quintessential entrepreneur. But I reached a point where what I had created had to be managed. For many years it was about the next big sale—and don't get me wrong, the next big sale is important. But in order to survive past the five-year mark, you have to engineer scalable growth that is sustainable—and doing that takes a manager. Over time I learned that skill, but I found it hard and it went against my nature. I asked for help from some great mentors, including Steve Forbes and Ted Turner, who helped me build my business while still maintaining my entrepreneurial sensibilities.

In 1988, when I was first starting out, the very first company I sold an ad to was the Bama Companies. Although you might not recognize the name of the company, you have come face to face with their products. Bama produces some of the country's most recognizable products for the nation's largest restaurant chains, including pizza dough, breadsticks, hand-held baked apple pies and biscuits. The CEO of Bama at the time was Paula Marshall. She had just taken control of the company a few years earlier from her father, who built Bama through the 60s, 70s and 80s. Since assuming control, Paula has grown the company to a $200 million business by adding new customers, building new plants and expanding to China. Paula's experience casts her as the ultimate executive to my entrepreneur.

In 2009 Paula approached me about writing books and becoming a speaker. She was unsure if people would want to hear her story, or if she even had anything to say. I told her that I didn't know anyone else who had inherited a business in the 3rd generation, grown their client list to include some of the giants of modern commerce, expanded to China, and lived to tell the tale. I told Paula her experience read as the five-, ten- and twenty-year goals taped to most business people's bathroom mirrors.

Paula has an amazing story and is able to shed light on some of business's greatest challenges. This book emerged out of several conversations with her about the common problems most business people face, whether they are entrepreneurs or executives. We finessed the timeline a little in the book to make things more interesting to read, but ultimately, reading this book should feel like becoming a fly on the wall while two business people from very different backgrounds discuss the issues of building a successful enterprise.

My main hope is that people from both worlds—management and entrepreneurship—can learn something from each other by reading both of our perspectives. In order for American business to flourish, we have to bridge the gap between entrepreneurship and management, and the only way to do that is by talking to each other and learning from what each of us has to offer. I hope you will find this book to be a jumping-off point for you to start some of these conversations on your own.

Now, with most things in life, we aren't usually one-hundred percent on one side of the fence or an other. For example, an executive can have entrepreneurial characteristics and vice versa. However, I have found that most people lean one way or the other. To help you gauge where you are on the spectrum, take the quiz on the following pages. We have developed it to help you determine what percentage Executive you are and what percentage Entrepreneur you are. Knowing this information will help you tune into what areas you need to strengthen in order to become more successful in business.

At the end of each chapter is a Learning Toolkit. Since the material discussed in the chapters is mostly theoretical, the Learning Toolkit will give you ways to practically apply what you've learned. The toolkit has two parts—one part is for the executive practical applications, and the other part is for entrepreneurial practical applications. Revisiting your quiz score will let you know which area you need the most work on, though it is always beneficial to know both sides of the coin.

Jim Stovall

Are You An Executive or an Entrepreneur? Business Style Quiz

Circle the statement that is **most** like you. In some cases it may seem both statements describe you, but please choose the one that is most appropriate, even if it's by a close margin.

---

1. A. When I see a situation, problem or need for something, I think, "Somebody should do something about this."

    B. When I realize there is a need for something, I try to come up with ideas or solutions; I view it as an opportunity worth pursuing.

---

2. A. People say that I am a planner. I have to have a well-thought-out plan for everything. I am calculated in my thoughts and actions, and I always know what to do next.

    B. People say that I am impulsive and can seem scattered. I don't consciously plan—being spontaneous is important to me.

---

3. A. I am good at figuring out what people want and making sure they get it.
    B. I am good at making people passionate about my ideas and visions.

---

4. A. I do not like change—I strive to make sure there is little change in my life.
    B. I thrive on change; not knowing what comes next excites me.

---

5. A. I am risk-averse; it takes a lot of convincing before I will take risks.
    B. I like to take risks and seek out opportunities to do so.

---

6. A. I pay meticulous attention to detail.
   B. I am a big-picture person—I just like to know things are getting done to get me closer to my goals.

7. A. I focus on one task at a time until I feel it is completed.
   B. I multi-task, sometimes juggling eight or nine things at once.

8. A. I want to like my job, but work shouldn't be everything in life.
   B. It is important to me to love what I do. I consider what I do integral to who I am.

9. A. I need to have a lot of money in savings to feel comfortable.
   B. I can live on a shoestring as long as I am happy.

10. A. I work best when I have lots of people around to bounce ideas off of; teamwork leads to a better end result.
    B. I work better alone. I often come up with my best ideas when going through my daily routine.

Scoring Your Results

Add up the number of As and Bs you marked. Take your A score and multiply it by 10. This number is your Executive Percentage. For example, if you marked 6 As, you are 60 percent Executive. Now do the same with the number of B answers.

Interpreting Your Results

Usually we find that most people lean heavily toward one side or the other. For example, a score of 40 percent Entrepreneur and 60 percent Executive implies that the person may need to work a little on their Entrepreneurial skill set in order to better complement their Executive skills. However, every once in awhile someone comes up with an exact 50/50 ratio of both mindsets. In this case, it's important to know that a) you are in the minority and are very lucky, and b) it would be good for you to try to hone both skill sets, as you are very balanced. Most of us should strive to reach a 50/50 balance in our lives. This does not mean changing who you are—it simply means learning to tackle problems in new ways. Different situation will call for different approaches and that is why it's important to be as balanced as possible.

Chapter 1
Building the Ship

As I stood in line to take my driver's test, I knew without a doubt that I would not be able to see the eye chart. It didn't matter. Nothing was going to stop me—I was going to be driving. I was sixteen and nothing was going to hold me back, not even my own eyes. The small matter of seeing what I was doing would have to wait. I was next in line, and had to figure out something fast. I listened closely to the guy in front of me as he read the chart and memorized every letter. Then, suddenly, it was my turn.

"Name please," the examiner said.

"Jim Stovall." I stepped up to the mark and repeated the letters just as the guy before me had stated them. I said them slowly, for dramatic effect and to seem as if I was reading them myself.

"That's amazing!" the examiner said. "I've been giving this test for 17 years and I've never had two people miss the same letters twice in a row."

I was cool as a cucumber, and since the guy in front of me passed, so did I. I received my license and went along my merry way. I didn't let it leak to a soul that I couldn't see all the details of the road. I figured as long as I could see the other cars coming and going, I would be fine. It couldn't be that complicated.

Two weeks later I crashed into the back of a parked police car on a fairly empty street. My car was totaled. I had saved up all summer for that car, unlike a lot of my friends whose parents bought their cars. I was humiliated when I had to call my dad and tell him that I was standing on the side of the road with a cop, and that I had just crashed my car into his. I wasn't hurt too badly—other than my pride. I never drove a car again. I had to kiss my "Summer of Love" goodbye. But more importantly, I had to come to terms with the fact that my vision was getting worse. I had been putting off going to the eye doctor for months. I was busy with football and school—besides, what's the worst that could happen? They would give me contact lenses. Or glasses. Or bifocals. They would help me.

Sitting in the chair at the optometrist felt like an eternity. Charts were being whisked around, x-rays were put up and then taken down, experts were pulled in and out of the room. The one constant was me. I sat, wondering if this much activity was normal for a routine eye exam. As the activity slowed to a halt, a doctor zeroed in on me.

"Jim—we don't know why, and we don't know exactly when, but we know without a doubt that someday you are going to go blind, and there's nothing we can do to stop it," he said.

I was speechless. Three words changed the landscape of my world forever: Juvenile Macular Degeneration. That was the evil monster coming to steal my sight; it wanted to take my freedom, my opportunity for a college scholarship and most importantly, it wanted to rob me of my chance at having a normal life. I was seventeen and had my whole life ahead of me, yet my whole world came crashing down.

So, I did what any strapping, strong Oklahoma boy would do: I ignored the problem. I told myself they were wrong, that they'd made a mistake. I wasn't going to go blind any more than anyone else around me. I continued playing football as if nothing was wrong, and I didn't tell anyone I had a vision problem. It was just like it wasn't there. But inside, I was scared.

As my vision deteriorated, I continued to pretend there was nothing wrong. I went on to join the Olympic weightlifting team and compete at that level. I knew that football was a lost cause for me, so I picked up weightlifting *just in case* the doctors might have been right about the blindness. I wanted to be the strongest blind guy the world had ever seen.

I went on to college, and by my second year I had to have a reader on standby to read me my textbooks. I could still see the professors moving around at the front of the room—they were blurry figures with gestures large enough for me to distinguish them from the blackboards behind them. It was around this time that I started acknowledging the fact that I was going to lose my sight. But I wanted to prolong the inevitable as long as I could. With the thoughts creeping in—the realistic thoughts that I was actually going blind—I decided that I had better spend some time with some blind people to understand what it might be like for me.

I began volunteering at a school for blind children. I told the principal about my condition and I decided it would be nice if they let me teach some of the kids. I had never taught anyone before, or been around blind children before, but I thought it was a good starting point. The principal thought differently, and she laid out another option for me. They had one student who was causing a ruckus for the other children in his class. Christopher was four years old. He was blind, and had several other physical problems. It had been determined by his teachers and the principal that he would never learn more than he already had. My job was to keep Christopher away from stairs—stairs can be very dangerous for blind people, and they were especially dangerous for Christopher—and to keep his shoes tied. He didn't know how to tie them, and since it had been decided that he would never learn how, someone would have to make sure they were tied all the time. Shoes tied. No stairs. That was it. They wanted me to keep him quiet because he was causing disruptions in his classes and keeping the other students from learning.

As a college kid who was facing a world that was getting darker and darker every day, I thought it was wrong that so much had been determined for Christopher without his say. When I met him for the first time, I sat down next to him and told him, "Christopher, if you don't learn anything else from me being here, I want you to learn how to tie your shoes and how to climb the stairs."

"I can't," he said in a small defeated voice.

"Yes, you can," I told him.

"No, I can't," he said again. We went round and round on this deal, as four-year-olds sometimes do, and I decided it would be better to show him than tell him that he could.

I continued attending my classes regularly and getting all my work done so that I could head over to the school for the blind in the afternoons. I made it my mission to teach Christopher these two basic life skills. As I neared my graduation, Christopher was getting better and better. As soon as he believed that he could do it, he began to improve.

My sight had finally deteriorated to the point that I couldn't get around by myself anymore. I was feeling especially defeated and depressed. I just didn't think I could go on like this. Who was I kidding? What was I going to go on and do? Most of the things I was learning in school were meant for sighted people. I didn't even know what was going to happen to me after graduation. Feeling very low, I decided that I was done. Done with college and done with trying to lie to Christopher and teach him how to have a more normal life. I headed over to the school for the blind and went into the principal's office.

"I quit." I even sounded convincing to myself. "I can't help Christopher any more. I can't even get around on my own."

The principal let me out of my obligation with little resistance. What I didn't know was that Christopher was sitting in the office, waiting to talk to the principal. He had been listening to our conversation. As I walked out of the office he trailed after me.

"You can't quit," he said. "What about my shoes? What about the stairs?"

"I just can't do it, Christopher," I said, utterly defeated.

"Yes, you can." His small voice repeated back to me what I had told him a few months earlier.

I felt rocks in the pit of my stomach. How was I going to explain to this kid that I was quitting, when he had been blind his whole life, had been told he'd never even tie his shoes, yet continued to show up and try to learn every day? I had a realization right then and there that changed my life. I could either step up and stop trying to quit in my own life—or I could stop lying to this kid. If he could do it with tying his shoes and climbing the stairs, then I could do it in my life, too. I could keep going.

My depression wanted me to lock myself in a room in the back of my house and shut out the world. My denial wanted me to surround myself with only the things I knew so I wouldn't have to face the petrifying fear of the outside world.

But kneeling down to speak to this four-year-old boy about why I wanted to quit life, I realized I couldn't do it. I couldn't quit. I wouldn't quit. I owed it to Christopher and to everyone in my life who loved me.

I went on to graduate college with two degrees. One of the last things I remember seeing—really seeing—was Christopher climbing the stairs, turning around, sitting on the top step, and tying his shoes. We had both accomplished the goals we set out to, and had proved something to ourselves.

~~~~~

Even though I had graduated and admitted to myself that I could still accomplish my dreams as a blind person, the road ahead would not be an easy one for me. I woke up one morning not long after graduation, and even though my eyes were open, there was no difference from when they were closed. I got out of bed, carefully counted my steps to the bathroom, and turned the light on. No change. I had lost all sensitivity to light. I had gone completely blind. It had actually happened. While I had been ready for this for a number of years—secretly fearing it every morning—it was a completely different feeling when it actually happened.

I was blind.

I am blind.

What am I going to do now?

Even after my inspiring experience with Christopher, I had to fight my own battles. My idea of safety and security was locking myself in the back room in my house with my phone, my desk and my tape recorder. I had a VCR set up with a TV and a stack of my favorite movies. I knew where everything was: the TV was four paces from the desk and six paces from the couch. There were no surprises.

I made that room my haven, and spent the next few months there, without any direction in my life. I didn't know what I could do, and was more focused on what I couldn't do. I spent most of my time listening to books on tape.

One day, I decided I wanted to watch a movie. I wanted something comfortable, something that I had seen a thousand times, figuring I'd be able to remember what happened at the points when there was no dialogue. I chose *The Big Sleep*. I am a big

Bogart fan, and with Lauren Bacall as the female lead, I was sure I would remember every detail. About a third of the way through the movie, somebody shot somebody else and I heard the screeching of tires—the getaway car.

The problem was, I could not remember for the life of me who had gotten shot or who was driving the car. Even though I had seen the movie a thousand times, I just couldn't jog my memory. Before I could stop myself, I uttered the words that every entrepreneur utters at some point: "Somebody oughtta do something about that."

Without knowing how, or even what I would do, I knew in that moment that I had to do *something* about this problem. After all, I was not the only blind person in the world. I was certainly not the only blind person who wanted to watch a movie and not get lost at the first sign of a getaway car. This was the first noticeable sign of a business plan. I didn't know where to go, but I knew I wanted to go somewhere. And somewhere was a new destination for me.

~~~~~

I had this idea stewing around in my head when I went to my first, and last, meeting of blind people at a support group called Vista. Over punch and cookies, I met a young lady named Kathy Harper.

"Nice to meet you, Jim. What do you want to do with your life?" I could tell Kathy was a no-nonsense kind of woman.

"Well, I have this idea. I want to create TV for blind people. I think if we could add an extra audio track over the vocal track that explains what's going on when there's no dialogue, then blind people won't get lost between conversations."

"When do we start?" Kathy asked. Like I said, no nonsense.

"Well, uh, it's just an idea for now," I said.

"Well are you gonna do it, or are you just talking about it?" That was the first time anyone had ever asked me that question. I thought about it.

"Well, why don't you meet me on Monday, and we can talk about how we can make this happen?"

She agreed.

~~~~~

We started Narrative Television Network out of that very conversation. In 1988, we rented the basement of an apartment building in Downtown Tulsa. Kathy still had some sight and was able to read. We began by emptying out an old broom closet and putting boat cushions on the walls. This was our very sophisticated sound studio. We started with the classic movies—the Bogarts and the Hepburns of the world. I was the narrator. Kathy was the technician. The way we worked it was Kathy would watch the movie along with me. I would have my script memorized and when it came time for me to fill in the plot with my narration, Kathy would poke me with a broomstick through a hole in the door. Very sophisticated.

We produced several tapes and found a sound engineer who was able to marry the new audio track onto the existing one. It seemed we were on our way. Until I realized we had forgotten something. This something was kind of important. How were we going to make money?

I thought that since we were going to have millions of blind people watching these movies we could sell advertising, just like the TV networks did. Kathy and I got in a cab and headed to the downtown library. We scanned the shelves until we found the book I knew could help us. With *The 100 Biggest Advertisers* under my arm, we left the library armed with the tool we needed to make some sales.

In the book I found the Bama Companies. I had always heard of the Bama Companies growing up in Tulsa—their pies were an institution. Bama is a large-scale manufacturer of frozen foods for companies like McDonald's. I had passed by their manufacturing plant throughout my childhood, the smell of cinnamon filling the air and making my mouth water. I recognized the name as soon as we found it in the book. I thought it was a good idea to start with a local company, and Bama seemed as good as any. I had Kathy read me the number, and I held my breath as the phone rang.

Learning Toolkit

Entrepreneurial Takeaways

Once Jim accepted that he was truly going to lose his sight, he decided to volunteer his time to help blind children. Rather than continuing to ignore the truth, he chose a way to learn more about his pending condition while simultaneously helping others. When he became discouraged, his commitment to young Christopher kept him from giving up. Many entrepreneurs become disheartened when they face obstacles to their goals, but looking to others for inspiration can go a long way toward bolstering your resolve and keeping you from abandoning your dream.

There is a critical moment when Jim says, "Somebody oughtta do something about that." Every entrepreneur speaks some version of this sentence at some point; it is what makes them realize they have an idea worth pursuing. Each time a person has this reaction to a problem, an entrepreneurial seed is planted. Pay close attention to any situation that prompts this reaction, as it may be the beginning of a business opportunity. Even though Jim didn't yet know where his idea would lead him, he was prepared for the journey and confident that there could be a good business idea here.

Jim recognized the need to solve a problem that directly affected him. In other words, he was squarely within his own target market. As a blind person, he understood the needs of the market to which he'd be promoting his idea. This can be critical to the success of a business because it gives the entrepreneur insight into customers' specific needs and desires, making marketing that much easier.

Kathy showed an immediate and passionate interest in Jim's idea, which he recognized as a valuable resource. Acknowledging talent and passion in those who are willing to support you is vital for entrepreneurs, especially in the start-up phase of a business.

Jim didn't let a lack of capital prevent him from pursuing his business idea. In true entrepreneurial spirit, he and Kathy started small, improvising a sound studio in an inexpensive space. This allowed them to turn out their product without needlessly spending money on an idea that was still in its infancy, and gave them a chance to see if the business was sustainable before making a major investment.

Executive Takeaways

As a teenager eager for a driver's license, Jim knew his poor vision would be a deterrent to passing the eye exam. Although his decision to copy the responses of the man ahead of him is questionable, it shows his ability to assess a situation and quickly find a solution to an imminent problem. Executives face split-second decisions every day, and need the ability to rapidly resolve problems and address unexpected situations.

When he volunteered to work with blind children, Jim disagreed with the school's decision that Christopher could not learn anything new. He told the boy that he would teach him to accomplish both tasks. Like a good manager, Jim recognized that teaching one thing at a time would get the best results, as opposed to expecting the boy to learn more tasks than he could reasonably handle.

Once Narrative Television Network was underway, Jim realized that somehow, the business had to make money. Sensing that advertising was the answer, he sought a resource that provided the information he needed to start marketing his company. An executive needs to know how to manage a business, starting with how to get the word out to potential customers or clients.

As soon as Jim settled on the Bama Companies as his first prospect, he lost no time in making the call. If he had hesitated, any number of reasons might have prevented Bama from accepting his pitch. Successful executives don't procrastinate, because they know holding off on a good plan can lead to disappointment and loss of business. In a sense, this is where the entrepreneurial spirit and good executive skills meet: the entrepreneur hits on an idea and the executive springs into action to ensure that it is carried out.

Chapter 2
Steering the Ship

I opened the cupboard again, hoping somehow for a different result. When I'd opened it five minutes prior, it had been empty save for a jar of jam and one piece of moldy bread. I closed the cabinet and walked away. But the hunger pangs would not subside, and neither would my hungry baby's cries. I creaked open the cabinet yet again, hoping that something miraculous had happened. Or maybe there was something in there I hadn't seen before. Something delicious hiding in the back. Alas, the same two ingredients stared back at me. Something had to change.

I went to my purse to see how much money I could find. Together with the food stamps, I was able to scrounge up eight dollars. That would be enough for the formula, but not much else. I began to mentally file through all the people I could call for help.

Jimmy—my husband. I hadn't seen him for a few days and last time he was in the apartment he threw a fit and took all the money he could find. He was in a bar somewhere, I was sure. Calling all the bars in the area wouldn't do me much good, since I was sure the money was gone anyway.

My mother. She hadn't spoken to me since I moved out of my parents' house. She was upset with me for keeping my baby and marrying Jimmy. She felt I was making a mistake. She told me that if this was the direction I wanted my life to go, she and my father wouldn't have any part of it. I mentally drew a line through her name—calling her wouldn't help much either.

My father—well, there's an idea. I kı ⌒w he didn't completely stand behind my isolation, but he felt helpless against my mother. He might've been the boss at work, but she was the boss at home and he knew what it meant to go against her. But I hadn't yet tried to approach him for help. Maybe I could ask him without my mom finding out. A plan began to form.

My baby girl, Cristi, was only a few weeks old. I had been struggling to pay the bills and get food on the table, but like all the women in my family, I am stubborn. I could not turn around and head back for home with my tail between my legs. That would mean that my mother was right, that I had made a mistake. And I could never believe that my beautiful daughter was a mistake. On the other hand, I could agree with her that Jimmy was a mistake. Throughout my pregnancy and the early weeks of our daughter's life, Jimmy had been intermittent. "Intermittent" isn't usually a word used to describe a person, but that's exactly what he was. When he was there, he was there one-hundred percent. "There Jimmy" made me believe that we could make this work, that everything was going to be okay. Then he would go away. He would either go away to work, or to look for work, or he would just tell me he was looking for work when he was really in the bar. "Gone Jimmy" was the one that caused all the problems. I never knew which Jimmy I was going to get. Today, with no food in the cupboard and a very short list of people to ask for help, I had "Gone Jimmy."

Out of options, I was ready to implement Plan Dad. I packed Cristi up in the car and stopped for formula on the way to my dad's office. I fed Cristi in the back of the car and hushed her to sleep. I stared up at the building that was my family's legacy. My grandmother, also faced with the challenge of feeding her children—but forty years earlier in the shadow of the Great Depression—began baking pies for the Woolworth's Drug Store in Waco, Texas. Word spread fast in a little town that was lacking in good news. Alabama Marshall made the best pies in West Texas, and probably the world. Lines formed around the block day in and day out. My Grandmother Bama kept right on baking those pies. Eventually she realized that she needed to create her own business—there was no need to keep giving all her profits to the Woolworth's. She, her husband, Henry, and their six children began what is now known as The Bama Companies, Inc. My father grew up to become a route man. He drove the trucks and delivered the pies to each convenience store, restaurant and home that had ordered a pie for that day.

Each of the six children came into the business in their own way. Aunt Grace opened a Bama Pie Shop in Oklahoma City in the 1930s and brought my dad up to work the routes in Central Oklahoma. By that time, my grandparents owned a pie shop in Dallas and my uncle owned one in Waco, in addition to my aunt's shop in Oklahoma City. My family was beginning to create a Pie Empire. But little did they know that this was just the beginning.

My dad stumbled in to work one morning, ready to pick up the pies for the route when he was blindsided by what he called "the most beautiful eyes he had ever seen." My mother, Lilah Drake, a local neighborhood girl, had gotten a job in Grace's pie shop. She was rolling out dough the first time my father laid eyes on her. She had never had a boyfriend before, even though she went to many of the church dances. When she saw Paul Marshall, though, it was love at first sight. It took my dad a few weeks to get up the courage to talk to Lilah, but once he did, it didn't take long for him to propose. The two were married and decided to open their own pie shop in Tulsa, Oklahoma.

Mom and Dad continued to build routes and deliver pies, as my Grandmother had done before them. Business was good, and my mom gave birth to my brother John shortly after moving to Tulsa. They were a happy pie-making family. In 1965, my dad had an idea. He went by the new drive-in in town to sell them some pie. They gave him the cold shoulder. "We need something people can eat in the car," they said. "Something they can eat with their hands." He headed back to the pie shop and told the ladies on the line that he wanted them to try something.

"I want to try to make a hand-held apple pie," he said. "Let's use the same crust and the same filling, just smaller and make it rectangular." He worked long into the night. His ladies from the line stayed a few extra hours, but they headed home after the first few batches failed.

"Mr. Marshall, what's wrong with our pies the way they are? Everyone says they're the best in town!" they said on their way out the door.

He didn't make much of an answer. He just kept working.

The result was a fried hand-held apple pie. It was unlike anything the world had ever seen. My dad thought he really had something here, but he would have to see if he could move any. He went back to the drive-in with a few of his new pies frozen in a cooler. The manager came to take a look at the new product. He told my dad that he wanted to put them on the menu, as well as any other flavors he had ready.

My dad was glowing with the opportunity of his new product. He began selling the hand-held pies throughout the Midwest; the delivery routes were growing daily. One day, heading back from a sales call, he followed signs to Chicago. He set his sights on the fastest-growing restaurant chain in the United States: McDonald's. Bama didn't have the capacity to deliver on an order for McDonald's, but my dad didn't care. He knew McDonald's would love the product, so he decided to go on a cold call to their offices in downtown Chicago.

He lugged his cooler up to the 39th floor of a skyscraper. He showed the product to the frozen food buyer, who agreed that McDonald's needed a dessert, and that this pie could fit the bill. Over the next few years my dad and the dedicated team at Bama developed a product specifically for McDonald's. A few representatives from Chicago came down to meet with the bank and co-signed a loan for Bama to build a large-capacity manufacturing plant. Bama went from selling a few hundred pies per day to selling thousands. My mom and dad had worked night and day to provide for us, and suddenly they had built a huge company whose product was being eaten thousands of times per day. The game had changed.

And here I sat, the seventeen-year-old daughter of my hard-working, successful parents who had built their dream out of thin air. I sat in the back seat of my car, feeding my new baby, with my life a mess. Could one cold call or one great idea change everything for me? I didn't feel like it could. I felt low, having to ask my father for help. He had pulled himself up by his bootstraps. He would be ashamed of me for giving up so easily. But what else could I do? I figured I would just ask him for some money, or for a leg up. The plan was to ask him and then get out of there as fast as I could. I didn't want to run into my mom. I knew she would talk my dad out of helping me if she knew what was going on.

I didn't know it then, but just like the moment my grandmother decided to make pies for herself, and the moment my dad had the idea for the hand-held pie, this was the moment that would change my life forever.

~~~~~

I carried my now sleeping baby quietly into my dad's office. He sat looking over paperwork and bills, and as soon as he saw me come in, his face brightened. I could tell he had missed me since I left home, and I had missed him, too. I was always a daddy's girl.

"Hey, there's my girl!" he said. I put my finger to my lips to signify that the baby was asleep.

"Hey, Dad!" I whispered. "She just got to sleep; she's been fussing all day." I left out the part about her not having any food, which may have contributed to her fussiness.

"Well, it's good to see you two," he whispered. "We miss you around the homestead."

"I miss you guys, too."

"How is it being out there on your own?" he asked.

This was a perfect lead-in, I thought. "Well, it's kind of hard. Harder than I thought. We're just really struggling with money." I braced myself for the typical "When I was your age..." speech. I knew he was going to tell me to buck up. That things could be worse. I didn't want to delve into the details of why things were so hard. My dad already didn't like Jimmy and I didn't want to give him a reason to chase him down with a shotgun.

"Well, it's funny you say that. We just had an opening down on the floor this morning," he said. He eyed me, waiting to gauge my reaction. I was floored. My parents hated, absolutely hated, entitlement. I didn't even think the possibility of a job was on the table because it seemed like taking advantage. They had made it through the Depression on true grit and hard work. My mother went back to work baking pies just two days after giving birth to my brother because she had to put food on the table. These were the kind of people that didn't give handouts. I just expected to ask for fifty bucks so that I could make it to the end of the week.

"I, uh, well... that would be great," I sputtered. "But what about Cristi? I can't afford anyone to take care of her..."

"Remember Melinda? Your nanny? I think she's gotten lonely since you kids grew up. Maybe she'd like to help you with Cristi. Your mom and I have been helping her out the last few years, since she's been in retirement. I'm sure we can make it work." I could not believe my ears. My dad was offering to give me a job and help out with childcare. I had not expected this. I was in tears before I knew it—tears of gratitude.

"Don't start that blubbering. Give me a few days to get everything worked out with Melinda and you can start on Monday," he said.

~~~~~

I showed up for my first day of work at 4 a.m. My schedule ran from then until 2 p.m.—a ten-hour day. I worked four ten-hour shifts a week. The work was grueling. I worked on the manufacturing line, placing frozen pie shells into the pie racks. The floor was loud and filled with machinery that could malfunction at any second. We wore hairnets, headphones to block out the noise, and frock coats. My typical day was filled with repetitive motions: fill the pie rack with pie shells, roll the rack into the huge freezer, pull another empty rack, repeat. If for some reason the line was shut down for a few hours, we had to clean. We cleaned everything from top to bottom every chance we got. Even with all the protective covering, it was still deafening in there. You couldn't talk much to your fellow employees without screaming, so most of us just kept to ourselves. Except during our lunch hours—the lunch room became almost as deafening as the plant because of all the chatter. The workforce then was mostly women—a lot of them were Hispanic, Asian-American and African-American. There were lots of different languages floating around, but all of us wanted to say our piece because we knew that once we were back to work, we wouldn't be able to speak freely over the machines. The machines did all the talking after the bell rang.

Ten years and two kids later I sat in the board room with my two brothers and my parents. I had worked my way up through the company, holding every position we had available, and in January of 1985 I found myself in upper management. My mom and dad were ready to get out. My dad had been in this business since he was just seventeen. He was tired and ready to move on—to Florida, for a daily regimen of golf. The question on the table was who was going to succeed him. i or the past ten years I had worked in every department from purchasing to shipping and receiving. What had started as a temporary job to help me get on my feet turned out to be a career and one of my passions in life.

My oldest brother John had worked at Bama most of his life, but he was facing major heart problems. The doctors strongly recommended that he not be put in high stress situations. My other brother had no real interest in the company. So that left me. I was there, working every day, and I had the experience. I seemed like the clear choice. But I was a woman. And I was young—32 years old, to be exact. Not only was I the best choice for the position, I really wanted it. But I also knew that proving myself to our employees and more importantly, to our customers, was going to be a long road.

My mom and dad announced to our family that I was being named the general partner of Bama. I was to be named the CEO and replace my father at the helm of the ship. I was both excited and terrified.

I gathered about 55 people, most of the management team at the time, and told them that I was going to be in charge of the company going forward. Many of them were happy; they had watched me grow up and I had been in management for a few years. They felt confidence in me that I am not even sure I felt in myself.

My main goal was to make sure that nothing changed. As a new leader in the organization, I had to keep things stable and keep the faith of my employees. At that point in time we had one great customer, McDonald's, and no debt. Being a supplier to a huge corporation is a great place to be in business, and if you're taking over, your main priority is not to screw it up.

Not too long after I had taken my post as CEO, I had a shocking realization. I was writing a check at the grocery checkout lane—this was before all the computerized check readers—and I had to fill out all my information.

"Where do you work?" the cashier asked.

"Bama," I said, not divulging more than I needed to.

"Oh, that place on 11th street? You poor thing," she said.

"What? Why do you say that?"

"I've heard that's an awful place to work. I heard someone's finger got cut off in the pie dough, and they made the pies anyway, finger and all!" She was almost as horrified as I was. I grabbed my groceries and hurried out of the store. "We have a problem," I thought. "We have an image problem." This was before terms like "public relations" and "brand recognition." All I knew was that we had a problem, and I had to fix it.

I had a friend, Helen Inbody, who was in job transition. She had run PR campaigns in the past. I created a position for her in a new department that I called "Community Relations." We decided that we needed to turn Bama's image around.

"Well, Paula, there are a lot of ways to skin a cat. How do you want to do this? Of course, we can buy your image in six months by giving millions to charity—or we can spread this out. We can start with little seeds to lots of different organizations and start an employee volunteer program. Of course, that would be a longer process, but I think it's more effective in the long run," Helen said.

"Well I think spreading it out would be our best bet, and save me some money to boot," I said with a chuckle. "What are your ideas for charities to give to?"

"Well, I just got a call today from an acquaintance of mine. He is starting a new company called Narrative Television Network. He is producing movies and TV shows with an extra audio track so that blind people can watch them and understand what's going on. He's actually blind himself. He wants us to advertise on the videos he mails out to the blind. The advertisements are $1500. I think it's a good place to start, and I'll look into other organizations that we can help," Helen said.

"Narrative Television Network, huh? Sounds like a great place to begin. What did you say the fellow's name was that started it?" I was curious. A blind entrepreneur—seems like you don't run into one of those every day.

"Jim Stovall, he's an amazing guy," she said.

"Okay, will you call him and tell him yes to the advertising? And then also see when there's time for us to get together. I'd like to meet him."

Learning Toolkit:

Entrepreneurial Takeaways

Seventeen-year-old Paula opened her kitchen cabinets repeatedly, *hoping* for a different result. Doing the same thing in the same way will result in the same outcome. Hoping and wishing will not get the job done. Recognizing that something has to change and taking action will.

Alabama Marshall did what she needed to do in order to feed her family during the difficult years of the Great Depression. She did the practical thing by taking a job, but utilized her passion and skill as a baker to create that opportunity. The unique skills and talents of an individual are generally undervalued by that individual. Recognize a skill or talent as a valuable, marketable resource, particularly when others show an appreciation or willingness to pay for it. If you're using your unique talents to the ultimate financial benefit of someone else, remember Grandma Bama. Eventually she realized that she needed to create her own business—there was no need to keep giving all her profits to the Woolworth's.

Though the Bama Pie Shops were already a huge success, Paul Marshall saw an opportunity for improvement and growth when the owner of the drive-in told him he needed something people could eat in the car and with their hands. He could have just accepted "no" for an answer, but instead, he reinvented his product, creating hand-held pies that were unlike anything the world had ever seen. The entrepreneur in him recognized that there was a need and a market already in place for this product.

Without everything in place, and without a plan, Paul Marshall drove to Chicago on a cold call to the fastest-growing food chain in the country. His decision to approach McDonald's, even though his company was not equipped to handle the volume of orders from such a client, is classic entrepreneurial behavior.

Entrepreneurial Takeaways continued

By being hands-on and working every position within the company, Paula not only learned the business, but developed a passion for it. When owners are involved and knowledgeable about all aspects of their business, they become attached to it on an intimate level. At the same time, as a business grows, business owners must be willing to let go of some of the tasks they are accustomed to doing, and trust that the systems and procedures they put in place will allow others to perform them just as well.

Paula chose a more unconventional, long-term process to alleviate Bama's image problem. Instead of throwing huge sums of money at it, she was open to new ideas, paving the way for Bama's relationship with NTN and Jim Stovall. Having leadership with a mindset that is adaptable and open to possibility creates increased options for businesses in terms of growth, expansion and partnership. Paula's natural curiosity in learning more about something that interested her forged a meeting that would probably not happen in typical managerial scenarios.

Executive Takeaways

Once Paula accepted that she needed help, he didn't randomly make calls or roam the streets. She made a mental checklist of the people she could and could not realistically turn to. She assessed the options available to her before making a decision on how to proceed. Taking the time to think about viable options and approaches before implementing them will save you and your company precious time and money.

When Alabama Marshall realized that her pies appealed to hundreds and hundreds of people in her local area, she came to the reasonable conclusion that they would have widespread appeal beyond Woolworth's. She formed her own company, and using that as a business model, her children were able to open up their own pie shops. The structure and discipline of formulating and following the recipes allowed for greater expansion of the family business.

In accepting a low-level position with Bama, Paula was able to learn the family business from bottom to top. Her first-hand knowledge of all of the work involved in creating their products helped her to rise through the ranks and ultimately earn the position of CEO. When managers can relate to employees because they have "been there and done that," employee confidence is higher.

Paula's main goal as the new CEO was to keep things stable. The key to maintaining the success of Bama Corp. was to not change anything in terms of how the company was run, since it had no debt and a very elite client in McDonald's. From this viewpoint, the adage, "If it ain't broke, don't fix it," well applies.

As the CEO, when Paula learned that Bama had an image problem, she addressed it in an immediate, decisive manner, bringing on an individual who had experience in Public Relations who could develop a plan for handling the problem. While the entrepreneur brainstorms and confers with experts, when facing major situations, executives need to be decisive and resolute.

Chapter 3
The First Meeting

I sat there at the table, so nervous I was sweating. I was the first one to our meeting, which would become a trend over the years of our friendship. Paula is a great businesswoman, but she is not great at being on time. I was about to learn this. But I couldn't help being nervous. Paula had said yes to our advertising proposal; not only that, she was the first one to say yes. Ever. To anything. Our sale to the Bama Companies was our first sale ever as a company. And now she wanted to meet with me.

I wondered if she was upset in some way with what she had bought. I wondered if she was going to ask for her money back. I didn't know what to expect. Suddenly I sensed an energy in the room that hadn't been there before. She was there, I could feel it.

"Hi Jim, honey, how are ya?" a perky, sweet voice asked me. "It's nice to meet you, finally! Helen has told me so much about you and she said we just have to meet."

"Hi Paula, it's really an honor to meet you. I want to thank you for agreeing to the advertising deal we sent over," I said.

"Oh, we're so excited to do it! It's a great thing you're doing, this Narrative Television Network, that's one of the reasons I wanted to meet you. I just think what you're doing is great," she said.

"Well, thank you. I really believe that the 13 million blind people in this country deserve quality entertainment…" I started.

"Thirteen million! Wow! You know, Jim, I guess I just never thought about it. But I'm happy I could help, that's for sure. You know, the real reason I called you here today is that I think we could really help each other. I mean Bama is always happy to help a great cause like NTN, but I'm talking about you and me, personally. I think we could help each other," she said, wasting no time getting to the meat of the matter.

"How do you mean? From where I'm sitting, I'm the one getting all the help here!" I laughed, but it was true. What could I do as a struggling entrepreneur to help this corporate businesswoman? She made decisions every day that were worth more than my entire life.

"Well, I just took this post about three years ago. My father was running the company up until then. I am in the middle of my Master's Degree in Communications, but you know what I've found? I'm not learning half as much in school as I have from my colleagues and from my experience. To tell you the truth, I've always wanted to be an entrepreneur. I just admire entrepreneurs so much. It's so exciting. I don't think what I do is very glamorous. I just try to keep the ship afloat. But you, you're building the ship!" I could tell she was a passionate person.

"Well, yeah, you're right, but I think you're on to something here. As an entrepreneur, I am out there and if I don't sell something, I die. Your main goal is to stay the same; if I stay the same, then I die. We're coming from very different, but sometimes similar viewpoints. I think we could learn something from each other. The Entrepreneur and the Executive… I like that." I was genuinely interested in what I could learn from this enigmatic woman. And I always love making new friends.

"What does your typical day look like? As an entrepreneur, what are your priorities?" she asked.

"Well, it's funny you ask that. My associate Kathy and I just finished producing our first tapes. We found a way to marry the new audio track onto the existing tape, so we've produced a few old movies with these new tracks. So this way, when someone in the movie drives off in a car, or gets shot or something, it gets explained to the blind viewer, so that they don't get lost in the story. Once we had finished making these tapes we decided to set it up as a home video service, where people could order the tapes out of a catalog.

"We realized we were missing out on a huge monetary opportunity because we could sell ads on the tapes. You know, how when you see a movie on TV there are always commercials? We thought that we could sell commercials on the tapes for an additional revenue source. So, as you know, I've been trying to sell ads. When I come into the office in the morning, I pick up the phone and start calling. I call the national companies that are based here in Tulsa—hence why your office got several calls from me. I call and call and call. I call until they let me talk to the head guy. I say, 'Listen, I've got nothing else to do but call this number, so just think how much time you'll save yourself if you just let me talk to the guy in charge. It will only take a minute.' After awhile, they usually let me talk to him.'"

"Wow, Jim. It's all about chasing that almighty dollar right now, huh?"

"Of course! If I don't make that next sale, I can't tell you what tomorrow will look like. Every new sale looks like a bag of groceries."

"That's so interesting. That's how my dad was. He was the ultimate salesman. I think it's what he really loved to do. He was the entrepreneur in the family. Now that things have gotten so big and bulky, he's not interested in running it anymore. I find that with a lot of entrepreneurs. They are interested in starting things, in the adrenaline involved in going from sale to sale, but then when it comes to managing, there's a real shortcoming. Growth is good and important, but if you can't manage it, then it's going to go south fast." Paula was really in her element now.

"You're exactly right. But I'm so bogged down by the idea that I might not make that next sale that the last thing I want to think about is managing. At this point, there's nothing *to* manage." I laughed again, but I knew there was a need for some kind of transition from the entrepreneur's mindset to the manager's. "Well, let's take the heat off of me for a minute. What about you? What does your day look like? What are a manager's priorities?"

"Well, a manager's priorities are what I like to call CYA—Cover Your Ass." We laughed together.

"No, I'm just kidding. But my day looks like a lot of meetings. We have strategy meetings, execution meetings, and then we have more meetings to see if our strategy worked. I am traveling to Chicago a lot to meet with McDonald's. They are in a real growth period and we have to make sure we can meet the demand for our product. We're trying to decide if we're going to open another plant or not—so there are a lot of decisions to be made and factors to consider. That's pretty much my day-to-day life. Opening a new plant, though, that sounds more to me like being an entrepreneur than being a manager. It's exciting and scary at the same time. I haven't felt that kind of thrill as a manager, but there's also not as much security either. See, Jim, I can be entrepreneurial too!"

"You know, it seems to me that both of us are going to have to be both entrepreneurs and managers throughout our careers. I don't know if very many people understand that. If you just managed your business, without introducing the new energy and innovation of entrepreneurship, you would just manage it into oblivion. You have to add new products and new customers and new plants. If you're not growing, you're dying. If you let yourself become too risk averse, then your business cannot make it.

"However, on my side of the coin, I have to become a manager as well. I can't keep selling and selling with no way to reign in the infrastructure. At some point I have to deliver on what I'm selling these people. I have to build systems and protocols. I think this is why we came together today, so that we can understand each other's perspectives." The meeting had that feeling about it. There was something that brought us together.

"Well, I think you're right. We can't be the only people in the world that have realized this. Who else can we learn from? I want more Jims in my life!" Paula said.

"Well, I've been thinking about something. I want to build my 'Dream Team of Mentors.' I've thought about this a lot, and I think I've devised a way to contact some of my heroes in the business world. I'm going to write a one-page letter to Ted Turner. It's just going to say, 'I don't want to waste your time, but I have something I would like your opinion on. Please let me know when you can spare ten minutes in the next six months—if we have to meet at the South Pole at three in the morning, it doesn't matter, I'm there.' You know, you get the gist. It's an experiment. I want to see if these guys will respond to me, and maybe we can strike up a friendship—just like you and I have done here today. If it works with Turner, I assume it would work with any business leader. I just picked him because he's in TV and I want to go into TV."

"Wow Jim, that's a great idea. I'm no Ted Turner, but I think I would answer a message like that. Ten minutes is nothing! I think I'll try it with a hero of mine—Dr. Edward Deming. He's a god to the Japanese; they say he revolutionized their manufacturing systems. I'm attending a lecture of his in a few weeks, but I'll try the letter thing too."

"I know Deming. I think he would be happy to answer a letter like that from a manufacturing business owner. Well, this has been a delight. I hope you'll keep in touch with me and let me know how it goes with the new plant and with Deming and all." I went in for a hug, hoping I wasn't being too forward.

"Of course I will! We have to get together again soon, to keep this momentum going. And good luck with Ted Turner! Ted Turner, wow, I can't believe we're already talking about him like we know him." She laughed that infectious laugh that I'm sure has gotten her foot in the door at a lot of places. We parted ways with our action steps in mind, and I think we both somehow knew that something special had started at that lunch.

I went on to meet Ted Turner from a letter I sent him, just like the one I described to Paula. I am now lucky enough to call him a friend. I also sent a letter to Steve Forbes, of *Forbes Magazine*. We hit it off and now I routinely go and see him in New York to catch up. I don't know where I would be in my business today without the help and guidance of mentors like these. Every young business person should strive to learn from the best in their industry.

Paula went on to become a student of Deming's after our conversation. When attending one of his seminars, he requested that she come backstage and meet with his graduate students. She was able to sit in on some of his sessions and learn many practical manufacturing techniques that would improve the quality of her products. Later, in the 90s, Paula tried the letter-writing technique with another one of her heroes, Stephen Covey. Mr. Covey wrote *The Seven Habits of Highly Effective People*. After using this book for a few years in her management training sessions, Paula reached out to Covey and he also became one of her mentors. She ended up winning an award for Principle Centered Leadership, which Covey himself gave her.

I was proud that my letter idea worked and that we could both say we had some amazing mentors in our corners.

Learning Toolkit

Entrepreneurial Takeaways

Jim talks about Paula's lack of punctuality. While this seems like a minor point, the more important aspect is the focus on one's ability to be flexible. Everyone, executives and entrepreneurs alike, have some habits and traits that are less than desirable. Being adaptable to the imperfections in others, rather than rigid about your own expectations, can lead to discovering their assets as well.

Though Paula is an executive in a major corporation, her instincts as an entrepreneur are evident when she tells Jim that she thinks they could help each other. She could have simply handed over money for advertising to help improve the image of Bama. Instead, she was impressed by the concept of NTN and, as an excellent executive, recognized the skill set that must be involved with it and followed her instincts.

"If I stay the same, then I die," says Jim. Entrepreneurs recognize that the original concept of their business needs to grow and change to accommodate the wants and needs of their target market and to expand that market.

Jim was able to describe his typical day and priorities in just a few short sentences when Paula asked him. Entrepreneurs must be so intimately connected to their business that they can essentially give their "elevator pitch" to anyone at any moment in less than a couple of minutes, or the length of the average elevator ride.

Like Paula's father, Jim's priority was to let his target market know about his new product. He made cold call after call after call to speak to whomever he needed to in order to make the sale. Part of being an entrepreneur is not only developing a new product, idea or way of doing something, but having the passion and dedication to make others passionate about it, too. And Jim's belief that if he could just speak to the point person in charge of making decisions, he would make the sale, is a top-notch quality of the consummate entrepreneur.

Jim recognized that innovation is the key to keeping a business in the public eye. If you're not growing, you're dying. True entrepreneurs are not afraid to take risks— or even if they are afraid, they don't let that stop them. They expand and grow by leaving their comfort zones.

Jim allowed himself to think big. He decided to write to Ted Turner, one of the most successful men in his business, for advice. The worst that could happen was that he would get no response. Entrepreneurs think within the realm of real possibility, not fantasy. They are positive thinkers with "nothing ventured, nothing gained" attitudes.

Entrepreneurs generally seek out the guidance of mentors. They recognize that they can learn the most from leaders in their industry. They are confident enough to approach others for advice and to admit what they still need to learn.

Executive Takeaways

Being passionate and committed to a company or product is important, but managing growth, being organized, having direction and a system of checks and balances are necessary to keep things flowing smoothly. Paula described her typical business day, and though her schedule may not provide the adrenaline rush of building and selling, implementing systems and protocols, having staff meetings, developing strategies and meeting with clients to ensure satisfaction are essential to the company's success. Without the inherent traits of an executive, a successful business could easily end up out of business.

Jim knew that in addition to selling, he had to have a system for managing sales and delivering goods. A thousand orders after a week of phone calls doesn't amount to one thin dime if the product isn't manufactured, shipped, delivered, and the cost and profit calculated. The tedious/boring tasks of inventory and accounting aren't burdens to the executive—they are the tangible proof of success.

Paula recognized her responsibility and ability to manage the Bama Companies, as well as her true role as CEO. She keeps the ship afloat. But she also realized there is another side to business that would be fulfilling and exciting to her—the actual building of the ship. This is another prime example of the executive and entrepreneurial mindsets simultaneously at work.

While formal education is certainly valuable to one's profession, never underestimate the learning opportunities available in the form of colleagues and hands-on experience. Paula is a CEO in the process of obtaining a Master's Degree, but she places high emphasis on the knowledge she has gained from working her way up through the company and alongside her employees.

Entrepreneurial and Executive Takeaway

On both ends, the critical learning tool is actually taking the action step. Jim and Paula both left their first meeting with a plan of action. Executives can plan and conduct meetings, but without action, none of the plans will be implemented. Entrepreneurs can have a hundred ideas about how to develop and market, but without action, they remain simply ideas.

Chapter 4
Good Deal, Bad Deal

One morning while I was going through piles of mail, I got a call from Jim. It had been a few months since our last meeting and I had been meaning to call him, but of course, work was getting in the way. I had felt so energized by our meeting earlier that year that I had begun thinking about the duality between entrepreneurs and executives. I noticed that my thinking somewhat oscillated between the two mindsets several, sometimes maybe a hundred, times per day. I wondered if Jim was feeling the same way.

"Jim! Gosh, I can't believe it's been this long since our lunch. We're getting underway with the new plant and things are just crazy around here. How are things going with you?"

"Business is booming! I decided the subscription service just isn't enough. I want to be on TV; I want to be on a network." Jim sounded passionate and excited. He was so sure of himself and this huge move for his company, and I wondered if he was feeling any anxiety about the amount of risk he might be facing.

"Wow, Jim, that's amazing. How are you going to do it?"

"Well, it's funny you should ask that. I just got out of a meeting with a guy they call the 'Gorilla of Cable Television.' He sat and listened to my idea and all the nuances of it for about thirty minutes before telling me that no network anywhere would ever want to carry my content." Jim didn't sound upset about this.

"Last week, while I was waiting for the meeting with him, I got impatient. Patience is not one of my top ten qualities. Anyway, I headed up to Tulsa Cable Television with my box of equipment and tapes, and I asked to see the man in charge of programming. They took me up to his office and when I finished explaining my idea for a television network to him, he told me it was the most amazing thing he had ever heard. He told me they would put us on the air in thirty days! I just couldn't wait to tell you that story. So much for the Gorilla of Cable Television!"

His voice was ecstatic. I couldn't help but notice I felt a little jealous—Jim was out there doing real work, picking his company up and making it a success, and here I was drowning in paperwork.

"Jim, that's incredible. Are you going to try to sell more stations?" I asked.

"I think I will. I think I'll try to sell as many as I can. It's my dream to bring television to the visually impaired, and the more networks that pick us up, the more people we can do that for." He was energized by the idea of his dream taking off, and it made me energized for him.

"Can I be true to our pact and offer you advice from the other side? From the executive side?"

"Well, you just figured out the reason I called."

"Oh, good! Well, this is a huge opportunity for NTN, and for you. You could get so much more exposure and reach so many more people being on the networks. But I want you to think about it before you get too excited and jump into this. It's a whole new business model than what you've been doing. You've got to decide now, before you get too far into this, if this is a good deal or a bad deal.

"Now, I'm not trying to be another naysayer like that Gorilla man because I think you could sell to a ton of networks and advertisers. I think they would love to support your company. However, moving in this direction will change the trajectory of your company forever. You have to recognize that and make sure that the new direction will do three things: 1) make you happy; 2) fulfill the mission of the company; and 3) make you some money. I think it has the potential to do all three, but you have to decide for yourself."

"I know you're right, Paula, and that's why I called. I try not to let my emotions get too tied up in the business, but that's hard. I've been breathing this business, waiting for an opening in the clouds to tell me what the right move is. My heart is wrapped up in it. It's hard not to be overwhelmed by the excitement of this new direction. But it reminds me of something my grandfather once said. I was a teenager and I was just about to go on my first date. He sat me down on the couch and said, 'I can't tell you what's right and wrong, only you can decide that. But I think you should decide that here—instead of out there. Because sitting here on the couch with your grandfather, the world makes sense. Once you get out there with a young lady, the world won't make as much sense any more.' I need to decide what's right for NTN before I get so deep into this decision that I can't turn back."

"Exactly. I knew you would understand. Growth is very exciting. It's hard to take a step back and look at the negative side of things, but it's something we have to do as business owners. As an entrepreneur I would think that the pressure to make sales could outweigh your instinct to plan and be particular about who you work with. Do you think that's true?"

"Yes, of course. If I had enough money to coast for awhile, I wouldn't be too concerned about this next big deal. It's like being in a plane. Money gives you altitude, which also buys you time. Right now you're flying at 40,000 feet—if something goes wrong, then you've got time to find your parachute, or figure out what's wrong with the plane. As for me, I'm flying at 500 feet. If something goes wrong, or if I make a mistake, I'm dead. I don't have a lot of time, because I don't have a lot of money in reserves."

"That's right. But I'm asking you right now to try and operate with a 40,000-foot perspective. It will help you in the long run. Think about those three things I mentioned—will it make you happy? You have to be happy and healthy to run your business. Does it serve the mission of your company? And finally, will it make you some money—more money than if you put your time elsewhere?"

"Well, let me talk it out right now, with you—instead of out there..." he chuckled. "Me being happy and the mission of my company are one and the same. If my company's mission is being fulfilled, I'm happy. If more of the world's blind people are able to access television because of my company, then that is a big part of my personal fulfillment. So I think being on network television instead of working as a subscription service would increase our impact exponentially. And that makes me happy. And it fulfills my mission.

"As for the money—I believe that if you do the right thing, the thing that propels you forward, the thing that you are passionate about—then the money will come. The networks are willing to pay us for every hour of programming we provide. So I think that takes care of all three questions. To me, that sounds like a yes."

"Well, Jim, congratulations! It sounds like you just got out of the subscription business and into the television business. I can't wait to see what great things the world has in store for you!"

"Well, I didn't want to call just to talk about me; I heard about the new plant. Congrats!" I had forgotten about the new plant for the first time in months during this conversation. Now all the anxiety and excitement came flooding back.

"Oh, it's going to be great. We've negotiated the biscuit contract with McDonald's, so as soon as the plant is up and running we'll be making money. It's nice to have less risk. I mean, there's still *some* risk. It's going to cost millions just to build the plant and outfit it with all the equipment we need. I gotta tell ya, doing this plant is the most entrepreneurial I've felt here at Bama. My dad, even though he's fully retired, keeps calling to warn me against doing it. He thinks it's too much money and too much risk. It feels kind of good to make the decision without him. I think part of entrepreneurialism is being a rebel, don't you?"

"Absolutely. Just ask the Gorilla of Cable Television." He laughed again. "As soon as that man told me I couldn't do it… I swear there is no better form of motivation than someone telling you that you can't achieve something. Especially when it's something you care about, something you know can be done. I think it would be a shame to believe someone else about what we can and cannot do. Even if it's your teacher, your mentor or your own father, you can't believe someone else about your abilities."

"Jim, you're a great morning pick-me-up—better than coffee! Let me know how things go with the networks, and I'll be in touch too. Right now I'm staring down a mountain of mail that isn't going to open itself."

"I hear ya. We'll be in touch soon. And Paula?" He paused. "Thanks for everything."

"No, Jim, thank you!"

We hung up. I knew after that conversation that I had met someone who was ready to tackle the world head-on. He wasn't afraid of anything! I thought about my office and my team. We had lawyers and mediators and managers—all of us were afraid of everything. In a corporation, words like "million" and even "billion" get thrown around a lot. That much money makes people scared. I realized that fear is the number-one enemy of creativity, and no matter what business you're in, you have to be creative.

Although I intended to return to my pile of mail, I didn't. I just sat and thought. I thought, how can we eliminate fear in our corporation while still being acutely aware of risk? I wanted my team to adopt the freewheeling, thrill-seeking attitude of the entrepreneur at the corporate level. Well, I at least wanted them to be more fear-averse than they currently were. I began journaling in a notebook so that I could keep track of all the things I wanted to change at Bama, and ideas on how implementation of those changes might be possible. I also kept a running tab of the questions I wanted to ask Jim. On the first line of the first page, I wrote:

How can a big corporation learn to be more fearless?

Learning Toolkit

Entrepreneurial Takeaways

When Jim decided he wanted to pursue getting onto a television network, he asked Paula for her input before taking any definitive steps. Although he believed in his company and in his own abilities, he recognized the need to ensure he was making the right decision. Having a trusted executive in your corner is a huge asset for any entrepreneur. It's always a good idea to run your ideas by someone whose executive skills you value.

Jim acknowledged that he was overwhelmed by the excitement of his potential new path because it was an emotional move for him. As an entrepreneur, his company is close to his heart because it is a direct outgrowth of his personal experience and passion. He knew that he had to make a clear-headed decision *before* agreeing to take on the new project. Entrepreneurs often feel their companies are part of their identities because, like Jim, they have built their businesses based on their own interests and talents. It's easy to become emotionally attached and make a decision based more on your heart than your head; this is where it's wise to think like an executive, evaluating decisions and results objectively.

Because his business is so closely tied to his own emotions, Jim knew that although he had to make clear business decisions, he could not just disregard the personal impact of his business success. Knowing that his happiness and the mission of his company were linked, he saw that fulfilling that mission would increase his personal satisfaction. As an entrepreneur, it's important to acknowledge both sides of the issue: make your business decisions objectively, but realize that as the heart and soul of the company, your own happiness will also be affected by the outcome.

Jim realized how important money is in his decision-making process. Like most entrepreneurs at the beginning of their careers, he needed to make more money in order to keep the business going and be able to think about even bigger deals for the future. But money alone should not be the deciding factor in taking on a big responsibility. It's important to weigh all factors in order to be sure that income from your new venture will be worth the time and effort you'll have to devote to the project.

Being told by the "Gorilla of Cable Television" that his idea was no good, Jim was anything but discouraged. In true entrepreneurial spirit, he turned that rejection into the motivation he needed to prove his critic wrong. Almost every entrepreneur will be faced with a naysayer or two, particularly when they are starting out. Don't let negative opinions determine your goals. If you believe in your idea and in your ability to see it to fruition, keep looking until you find the person who likewise sees your potential. Like Jim, you know your own abilities; don't let someone else define them for you.

Executive Takeaways

Though she knew how excited Jim was about his prospective television deal, Paula's executive experience allowed her to guide him through thinking carefully about whether it was the best decision. When a new idea or prospect presents itself, it's important to decide whether it is a good deal before taking a leap forward. Some business decisions are real game changers that can alter a company's path, so it is vital to consider Paula's three questions and determine whether the new deal will make you happy, fulfill your company's mission, and make money.

As an executive in a financially secure corporation, Paula was able to encourage Jim to look at his new prospect from a different perspective. Most entrepreneurs operating with limited capital view their decisions as a road they are about to travel. Paula asked Jim to picture himself already at the end of that road, taking a look back. It's easy to look ahead and see a bright future, but a savvy executive will envision the end result and then consider whether the steps along the way merit the outcome.

Paula saw that, while an established corporation is obviously more financially secure than a start-up, that very security can instill a degree of fear. The huge sums of money involved in big business scare people because so much is at stake, and that fear can inhibit creativity. Paula knew that thinking in a more entrepreneurial manner could lead to greater creativity. As an executive, it's important to balance the corporate rules with some looser, more creative thinking. Yes, it's good for business, but it's also a key to personal satisfaction. Thinking outside the box and coming up with new ideas is a great way for executives to feel fresh and inspired.

Entrepreneurial and Executive Takeaway

The valuable takeaway for both entrepreneurs and executives is the ability to look at decisions and problems from the opposite perspective. Paula points out that her thinking vacillates between the two mindsets every day, and Jim is also learning the value of examining things from the other view. Entrepreneurs need the focus that executive thinking offers, and executives need the ability to think outside the rules in order to see the full picture.

Chapter 5
It Really is that Simple

fter that last call with Paula, things started moving quickly. We were getting calls from networks every day, all asking for our programming. About 30 days before we went on the air, a guy came into my office—he was what I like to call a "problem guy." He could make a problem out of anything; it seemed like he loved problems. If I told him I just landed a new contract with a network, he would come up with about 50 reasons why I shouldn't be happy about it. This particular day, he was the most harried I had ever seen him.

"We've got a huge problem!" he said. Typical "problem guy" behavior.

"Well, what is it?"

"The networks have given us two hours of airtime for our movie, but the movie only runs for an hour and a half. We've got a half hour of dead space. Once the networks see that, we're finished! And we don't have enough time to fix it!"

I could have sworn he was almost excited about our imminent failure. It was like he wanted to be proven right. He seemed to want confirmation that this problem was indeed huge enough to put us out of business. I sat and thought for a moment, then said the first thing that came to my mind.

"Well, I'll interview the stars from the movies we're showing, and that will take up the rest of the time." Of course, I had no idea how to reach these stars, or which ones I should call—and I figured it was quite a long shot that any of them would call me back. But standing there facing Problem Guy, I just couldn't let him win. I had to try.

Kathy and I went back to the library and this time we found a book called *Addresses of the Stars*. Some of them even listed their phone numbers. I knew that we had a Katharine Hepburn movie we wanted to put on, so once we got back to the office, I dialed the number as Kathy read it to me, thinking I would be directed to an answering service, or even a stock message for all the crazy people who were trying to call Katharine Hepburn.

"Hello?" It was the throaty, lyrical voice I would recognize anywhere. I was stunned.

"Uh, uh, hello. Hello? Is this Katharine Hepburn?"

"Yes, young man, it is."

"Well, this is Jim Stovall. You'll have to forgive me, as I'm a little surprised you answer your phone." I was struggling for my words.

"Well, don't you answer your phone, Jim?" She said it so matter-of-factly. This was the dry sense of humor I had always admired in interviews.

"Yes, yes, of course." I bumbled. "Well, I'm with Narrative Television Network. We provide programming for millions of Americans who are visually impaired. We are set to go on air in about a month on several networks, and I was wondering if I could interview you about your movie *Bringing Up Baby*. We would play the interview before and after commercial breaks. So what do you say, Ms. Hepburn?" I held my breath.

"I'll do it. Please mail me the details. It was nice talking with you, Jim."

And that was that. I couldn't believe it. Still stunned, I couldn't help but let Problem Guy know about what had just transpired. He chattered on about possible problems we might run into with logistics or some such thing, but I just walked back to my office, basking in the glow of my own ingenuity.

We continued calling the stars of the movies we were set to air, and once we told them that Katharine Hepburn was on board, they all agreed to be interviewed by me as well. The situation gave rise to what I call "The Katharine Hepburn Effect." I have since learned that this is an essential turning point for every entrepreneur. The Katharine Hepburn Effect is your first big client or advertiser or partner who has a recognizable and trustworthy name. Working with your first big name will build you so much credibility that many other trusted names will follow. That first person gets your foot in the door as a reputable business, and the business will snowball from there. It can all be traced back to that first credibility builder—for me, it was Katharine Hepburn. I've also realized something else since then: Paula, my trusted friend and confidant, was another one of my Katharine Hepburn moments. Bama was the first large company to advertise with NTN, so Paula was really my first Katharine Hepburn. I made a note to thank her for that when I had some time.

On that day in particular it seemed that Problem Guy was reigning supreme over my schedule. I had just been notified that there was another problem in the production room. We'd been running into a lot of mistakes down there, and they were all because of the same employee. I hate to admit that up until this point, I had never had to fire anyone. I had been extremely lucky with the staff I had hired, and it had just never come up. I honestly hoped that it never would. I think most entrepreneurs feel this way about firing. We'd been growing and adding new people every couple of years, and there had been a few minor issues, but everything seemed to smooth itself out. Now that I was seriously considering firing someone, I had no idea what to do. It looked like I had time to call Paula after all.

After a few days, Paula returned my call.

"Hi there, Jim. I saw that you called a few days ago, and I just couldn't wait any longer to call you back. Since the last time we talked, so much has happened! I know we meant to stay in touch more, but gosh these last few months have been a whirlwind." She stopped to take a break and I jumped in.

"Paula! It's so good to hear your voice! I know what you mean about the whirlwind. We've been pretty nuts here too. I have so much to catch you up on, but today I have kind of an urgent question for you."

"Well, I'm all ears."

"I don't know how else to say it, so I'll just ask: how do you fire someone? I mean, okay, I know *how* to fire someone, but… I'm having a hard time admitting to myself that I really don't want to do this." That was a little more transparent than I'd intended to be, but I needed her to know that I was… well, afraid.

"Jim, it's one of the hardest parts of being a business owner. I've struggled with it for many years and it never gets any easier. But I can tell you what we do here at Bama, and then you can adapt your own version for NTN. Is that okay?"

"Yes, I'm open to any help you can give me."

"Okay, well, as you know, at Bama we have a lot of employees, and we have these kinds of issues a lot. So, since we have so many people, we've had to kind of ritualize and build a process around termination. It becomes kind of laborious when you say it all out loud, but basically, here is our system: when we have someone step out of line or misunderstand their job description, our human resources team lets them know immediately. It's important to confront the problem early and head on, so expectations are clear. If an issue continues to come up, we bring in someone from upper management, and we have what we call a 'courageous conversation.' This conversation goes a lot deeper than just what the employee did wrong. It delves into the *why*. Are they having trouble at home? Are they abusing drugs and alcohol? Do they understand what is expected of them? Are they well suited to their job? We go into this conversation with a three-fold action plan: Intent, Behavior, Result—or IBR. We discuss the intent of the actions that caused us to have the conversation. Then we talk about the behavior itself, and how it could have been changed to reach a more effective outcome. Then we talk about the results. If the person is close to being terminated, we let them know that termination will be a result of their actions if they continue on this path. Then if the behavior continues, there is really no further step other than termination. It all gets very legal; because of our size, we have to watch out for lawsuits and things like that. No one wants lawyers to get involved. Now, in your case, I think things are much different. Your employees see you every day, they see you make decisions, so I think you are the one that has to carry out these kinds of talks."

"Wow. Your system is extensive, but it makes perfect sense. I like that IBR model. I may implement that in situations like this. In this case, it's time to let this guy go. He isn't right for the job and he's costing me money with all the mistakes he's making. I think the hardest part for me is threefold: not knowing what he's going to do, feeling guilty about letting him go, and wondering if there's anything I can do to help him improve before letting him go. I'd hate to go through all this when there's something I could've done differently to save this guy's job."

"Well, assuming you trained him properly and he's making lots of mistakes, I would bet that you're right—he's not right for the position. Also, Jim, one of my favorite sayings for this situation is, 'When is the best time to fire someone?' Most people rack their brains thinking about the times of year, or the times of day, but the answer is, 'the first time you think about it.' You know, because once you think about it, you're going to think about it again every time that person does something wrong."

"That's exactly what's happened in this situation. Once I thought about it, things just kept happening to prove my instincts were right."

"I've had situations where I've had to let someone go, and they ended up finding a job they really loved, or they ended up following a passion they'd had for years. It doesn't happen every time, but sometimes people are able to see being fired as an opportunity in disguise. And when you think about all the money you have to spend to run a business—and as owners, we get paid last— you are effectively paying this man to cost you money."

"Now that's an interesting way to think about it. I've been so busy thinking about how he's going to feel that I haven't taken time to think about how it's affecting my business and those people that work here that make this place successful. I've got to tell you, Paula, my right hand woman, Kathy—she's been with me since the beginning. She's also blind and we just found out that she's been diagnosed with terminal cancer. It's a tragic situation; we're all having a pretty hard time with it.

"She has a daughter, Jessica, who is just reaching school age and will have no one to take care of her when her mother passes. Kathy and I have agreed that I will become Jessica's guardian. She's going to become a trustee of NTN, which will provide for her college fund and future. When I think about that guy making costly mistakes, it equates to him stealing from a little girl who's about to lose her mother. That is not acceptable in my eyes. I think I'm ready to have that conversation now."

"I am so sorry to hear about Kathy. I know you love her. That is a great thing you're doing for Jessica. Gosh, how tragic. When you put everything in perspective like that, it makes your decision kind of easy, I would think."

"I mean, I guess it really is that simple. I can see that now. In a small business like mine, we don't have a lot of lawyers or procedures. We're pretty much a family. I've worked hard to make sure everyone who works here knows that. I can see now that to preserve my family and do right by them, I have to let this guy go. But up until now, it's been really hard to get to this point."

"I know it, but I think you're ready. Just think of Jessica."

Paula was right. If I was going to manage my business effectively, I had to know when and how to let people go. In such a small business, firing feels very personal. Many times, big companies create lots of legal paperwork and barriers so that the situation seems sterile and less personal. But when you get right down to it, no matter how big your company is, firing is hard. But you can't avoid it. Avoiding it will lead to a whole host of problems that you won't be able to manage. Just think of those people in your organization who have always done a great job, those who would do anything for you and your company—as a manager or owner, you owe it to those people to reward good behavior, punish bad behavior and eliminate those who just don't cut it.

Learning Toolkit

Entrepreneurial Takeaways

When faced with a potentially damaging problem, Jim voices the very first solution that occurs to him. Although he was able to make his plan work, this impulsiveness could well have backfired, costing him precious time to find an alternative solution. Being an entrepreneur is all about coming up with ideas, but it's important to carefully evaluate the possibilities before committing to a plan. On the plus side, however, he was not afraid to take the leap of cold calling a famous person to ask for help. This level of dedication to his business truly embodies the entrepreneurial spirit.

Once he decided to try contacting the stars of his movies, Jim knew he couldn't back down from the idea. Time is money in any business, and smaller companies in particular are often faced with pressing issues that require the owner's immediate attention. Doing some simple library research provided Jim with the tool he needed to pursue his idea.

Jim's "Katharine Hepburn Effect" represents a huge moment for a small business owner. He learned that landing the first big name, whether it's a client or advertiser or anyone who can positively impact your reputation, is a tremendous step forward. Word of mouth advertising is good for any business, but it's especially important for small businesses operating on limited budgets. Landing that first well-respected name will enhance your appeal to prospective clients.

Like many small business owners, Jim was reluctant to fire an employee. It's not uncommon for a small company to feel like a family, and for the owner to have a paternalistic attitude toward employees. But when an employee is not meeting the responsibilities of the job, it is the owner's responsibility to address the problem.

Jim acknowledged his own fears about not knowing how the employee would react, feeling guilty about firing him, and being unsure of whether he could help him to keep his job. Realizing that this might be an emotional issue for him, Jim made the right decision when he asked Paula for advice on how to handle terminating an employee.

Executive Takeaways

Based on her experience with a large corporation, Paula was able to outline a detailed process for handling disciplinary issues and terminating an employee. As an executive, she understands the need to look for the cause of the problem and to ensure that the employee understands the requirements of their job. Should termination become necessary, a formal process is in place to protect both the employee and the corporation.

Paula knows that the best time to fire an employee is the first time the boss recognizes that termination is warranted. Taking action right away eliminates the possibility of further mistakes or improper actions on the part of the employee. It also keeps the executive from feeling angry or upset with the employee's performance. In the long run, it is better for all involved to avoid prolonging the inevitable.

Looking at the bottom line, Paula recognizes that by keeping a poorly performing employee, a business owner is throwing money away. Not only are you paying an undeserved salary, you are in effect spending money for nothing, since the work you need done is not being fulfilled.

Entrepreneurial and Executive Takeaways

No matter what size your company is, taking disciplinary action and terminating employees is serious business. Unfortunately, it's something that every boss will have to face eventually. Jim and Paula both understood that avoiding the issue only leads to more problems, and that their good employees deserve to work in a positive environment, free of bad behavior and negative performance.

Chapter 6
The Promised Land

I was so excited I could barely dial the phone. My company, Bama, had been asked by McDonald's to open a plant in China. McDonald's had set their sights on expanding into China in the early 90s, and they wanted to use vendors they knew they could trust. Also, because of the state of China's economy at that time, there was really no one domestically that could produce the kind of products that Bama does. They had approached us about building the plant, and even though it was a very exciting proposition, I had to think hard about whether we wanted to break into the Chinese market. I knew I had to call Jim.

Up until this point in my life, I had always wondered if I could have done what Jim had done: start a business and build it from scratch—which is very different from taking over a business midstream. I had always wanted to know if I had what it took to do what my dad and Jim had done. But this China deal was the closest I might ever get to being a real entrepreneur. I was excited.

"Jim! Oh my gosh, I am so glad you answered! I think that you'll find the tables have turned…" I said cryptically.

"Well, that sounds ominous. How do you mean?"

"I am calling you because I need help…being entrepreneurial."

"My goodness—I can't wait to hear this!"

"Well, McDonald's has approached us about building a plant in China, just outside of Beijing. I'm so excited about the opportunity and the money, of course. This means a whole new era for our company. *We would be going global!* We've always been a domestic operation; our roots are here in America, and our products have always been American made. Now, the products made at the new plant would be solely distributed in China—they have a law that all suppliers must exist on Chinese soil. I have to be honest—I'm just scared senseless of doing this!"

"Well, you're not an entrepreneur until you're scared, that's for sure! It sounds like an amazing opportunity, but there are definit ly a lot of things to think about. You would be doing something that thousands of other businesses dream of doing. Let me ask you this: what does your dad think of this?"

"He's not too happy about it. He's been out of the day-to-day operations for quite some time and I don't think he has the right frame of mind about the idea. All he can think about is us doing business on foreign soil with communists. He's very afraid of what will happen. I don't understand it. He was like the original entrepreneur. He wouldn't think twice about this opportunity if this were 1961. It's like something's changed in him. He's so risk-averse now."

"You know, I think that a human's ability to take risks and live in fear is limited. And you know better than anyone else that your dad did it for a long time. I also think that when your family is depending on the next big deal, you're a lot more likely to take it. From his perspective, everything is peachy—Bama is making money. His thinking is, 'Why would you want to risk that in order to go overseas, where things are a lot less sure?' In a way he has a point, but I think his perspective is a bit dated. He's been out of the entrepreneurial game for a long time. And you're just getting started!"

"I see what you mean. He lived most of his life waiting for the next big deal. Not only because it gave him a rush, but because we needed it to stay alive. Now that he's in a 'safe place' so to speak, he would rather just stay there. But I honestly think that this is the best move for Bama. We can't risk McDonald's contracting someone else to do it, and the returns on the initial investment… well, they would be substantial and for many years to come."

"It's nice to think about the money, but don't get starry-eyed. It's important to consider the other factors too—the unknowns. Your dad is being a bit fanatical, but the Chinese *are* communist. What potential problems could that cause?"

"Well, I mean theoretically they could just walk into the plant the day it's completed and claim it as their own. They could seize all our profits as property of the government… there's really no end to what they could do. But from the way they're acting towards McDonald's, it seems that they really want American business to move in. Their economy is stagnated, and they need some new investors to get it moving again. I don't think they would risk that just to prove their dominance. The Chinese hate to be shamed publicly, and they know that if they did anything, it would be all over American television and radio. I honestly believe they want to partner with American businesses and do it the right way."

"Huh, that's very interesting. You have to learn so much about a country's culture and traditions before deciding to move forward and expand your business there. One thing I know, above all else, you have to trust your gut. If everything else seems wrong, but your gut is telling you to go for it, then you have to listen. I believe true entrepreneurs have an extremely well-honed sense of intuition. The most important thing is to be honest about time, talent, temperament and triggers. Before embarking on any entrepreneurial venture, ask yourself these four questions: Do I have the time necessary to devote to this to make it a success? Do I have the talent to be successful at it? Do I have the temperament to be successful—am I capable of making hard decisions, firing people and missing time with my family? And finally, will I pull the trigger? Because every venture like this will, at some point, get you out of your comfort zone. Whether it's a skill level you haven't attained, you need help that's not available, you want to do something you're not qualified for, or you have to risk some money that you wish you didn't have to. You have to be really honest with yourself and say that you would do all the things necessary to make this China deal a success."

I was quiet for a minute, soaking in Jim's words.

"Wow, at least I know I came to the right person! Time, temperament, talent and triggers. I just wrote that down, and I'm going to revisit that when I have some time to think. For me, something that is really obvious, and very scary, is that I have to trust these people, and trust that this will work out for the best. I have a great team. I know we have the talent and the time. I know we have the temperaments necessary to be successful. The one thing stopping me from pulling the trigger is trust. I know that sounds silly, using the word *trust* in a work environment, but that's what it is for me. I have to trust my team, I have to trust my customer who is gracefully leading the way, and I have to trust myself. This is the scariest deal I have ever done. I have dealt with multi-million dollar mistakes, massive customers, bad suppliers—but none of it compares to this."

"I would be lying if I didn't tell you this is a big deal. Every business person in the United States dreams of doing what you're talking about doing. It's the untapped resource, what most of us would call the new 'promised land'. You would be selling your products to almost a billion people who have been thinking about them and salivating over them for years. You're forging a new trail for American business."

"Well, when you put it that way, I just don't know if I can say no. But as you said, I have to think about some things before moving forward. Thank you so much for your perspective. It made me realize how different this venture is from just managing the company."

"You are so welcome, and I am so excited about what's to come for you! I'll talk to you again soon, I hope?"

"Absolutely!"

When I got off the phone with Jim, I was floored by the overwhelming information and perspective he had given me. Even though going to China was part of Bama, it was also its own unique entrepreneurial venture. I felt like I was getting one step closer to answering the question, "Am I a manager or an entrepreneur?" I began to realize that I, like every other business person, was both. You see, I think there is a daily oscillation between manager and entrepreneur that most of us don't even notice. Many managers would be ruffled and offended at the idea that they were entrepreneurial—being entrepreneurial could imply that you are flippant, indecisive, and as is often the case, broke.

On the flip side, I think that most entrepreneurs would balk at being called managers. Managers are boring; they rely on process and possess no real creativity or ingenuity on a day-to-day basis. These two schools of thought are considered different classes in business school, and different skill sets altogether. While I can't disagree that they are different skill sets, I think most of us carry inside ourselves elements of both. One thing is for certain: we have to employ both in order to properly start, build, manage and grow successful companies.

In that moment I was overcome with gratitude that I had met Jim, and that we could teach each other how to become the entrepreneur and the manager that we always wanted to be.

~~~~~

Bama went on to build the plant in Beijing. We installed an amazing team to manage the operations with all but two of the employees being Chinese. The Chinese love to go to McDonald's and they love the pies—however, their flavors are a little different. They have a popular Taro Pie, which is made from Taro Root and is bright purple on the inside. Bama has flourished from its relationship with China, but there have been a few hiccups along the way.

When we went into the country, we formed a relationship with a joint venture partner, one of China's biggest banks. We made the deal that Bama would put up $3.5 million as collateral for a $10 million construction loan. We would use the loaned money to build our new plant. We began construction and everything was going fine until I received a call about the bank holding my $3.5 million. It had collapsed, along with several other big Chinese banks. When I called the Chinese Government to get my money back, they said simply that they did not have it.

I was infuriated and having flashbacks to conversations I'd had with my father and Jim. They'd both warned me about dealing with a communist government. I didn't want to admit that my father had been right to be cautious. When my loan payment was due, I was floored by the fact that the bank representative actually called to ask me why I hadn't made my payment.

"Well, I haven't made my payment because $3.5 million of my money is gone!" I said, unable to hide my emotion.

As the translator conveyed this to the other person on the line, I heard silence. Then the bank representative simply repeated himself, asking for the payment again. I placed my phone on the hook, hanging up on the Chinese bank that had loaned me the money I needed to start construction on our plant.

Lawyers and bankers swarmed, trying to figure out who to call, what to do and how to get our money back. The Chinese banks never called us back. And so, as a response to their ignoring my requests, I decided I would not pay my loan payment. I called it my "Chinese Standoff."

I knew that if things went far enough, I would go to the American press and expose the Chinese for taking my collateral—the $3.5 mil—and it would be worldwide news. The Chinese economic collapse was kept very quiet—not like ours here in America. The last thing the Chinese wanted was publicity surrounding this problem. I held my breath and decided to wait it out.

After a few months, the calls from the bank stopped. I had gone about six months without paying my loan payment. In China, this offense would be punishable by jail time, but I knew that they would not press me much further. I had an instinct—what Jim might call a "listening to my gut."

I flew back and forth to Beijing with my Chief Financial Officer many times. We sat in the lobby of the bank and waited. We let them know we were there to see someone about our missing collateral. We sat and sat. No one ever came down to meet with us. Eventually we stopped making the trips. Other things became more important, and the economy in China began to pick up. We resumed construction on our plant and eventually we got a meeting with the bank where our loan was held.

We explained the situation about our missing money. They understood and were able to negotiate with us. We reached an agreement that made everyone happy, and like a good citizen, I began paying my payments again. Today we have three plants in China and all of them are running at full capacity. Because of my gut feeling, I didn't waiver when all that money went missing—and I was right about the Chinese not wanting to be shamed publicly. In the end, everybody won.

Learning Toolkit

Entrepreneurial Takeaways

Though the prospect of going global is exciting and will certainly produce tremendous growth and profit, Paula admits that she is "scared senseless" about opening a new Bama plant in China. Jim, the expert entrepreneur, knows that being scared is one of the key components of being an entrepreneur. Venturing into uncharted waters and doing things you've never done before is unnerving. The key is to accept the feelings of fear and forge ahead.

Paula is surprised that her father is not happy about the China deal. He had been the one who took chances and seized opportunity, but once safe and comfortable, he became risk-averse. What Paula comes to realize is that her father was operating from a different place and mindset when he was handling the company. He had grown and expanded Bama's business model because it was necessary, not simply because it gave him a rush. The drive behind entrepreneurs comes from their recognition that there is a need for something, but also from their own circumstances and need to generate income and be successful.

Paula sees the business deal in China as a huge revenue generator and doesn't want to take the chance that McDonald's would contract someone else to do what Bama had been doing for them for years. Taking the steps to grow with an existing client or partner so that partner doesn't find someone else has to be a concern for entrepreneurs.

Entrepreneurs trust their gut. In her conversation with Jim, though Paula was discussing the pros and cons of going into business with China, her instincts were telling her to go for it. Paying attention to that intuition, even while considering the options, is a key trait of entrepreneurs.

Entrepreneurs may not plan in as detailed a way as executives, but they do need to know the answers to specific questions about their time, talent, temperament and ability to take action. And they have to be honest about those answers to make taking the risk as low-risk as possible.

The entrepreneur in Jim sees the promise of Paula's business venture with China. Entrepreneurs see untapped resources for their product or service as leaving money on the table.

Executive Takeaways

Paula knows how to run a company. But she also knows that taking over the already-established family business and starting and building a brand new business by building a new plant in China are two very different things.

Even though an amazing opportunity presented itself with McDonald's wanting Bama to open a plant in China, Paula takes time to rationally think about her decision. She places a call to Jim because he is someone to whom she can go for expert information on being an entrepreneur. Managers and executives don't know everything; that is why they have employees and contacts. They utilize their resources to make well-informed decisions.

Jim reins Paula in from being too optimistic about the deal with China, encouraging her to consider the potential problems. Here is where his executive side is prominently displayed, as he and Paula weigh the pitfalls and positive aspects of Bama forging a relationship with China.

Paula realizes that building a new plant in China is a totally different venture than managing the company. She knows there is a lot of opportunity and possibility, but she is also aware of the risks and challenges. Unlike her father, who approached McDonald's all those years ago without thinking through how to handle a client of that magnitude, Paula's executive brain takes over before moving forward.

When the Chinese bank that gave Bama the loan to build collapsed, Paula utilizes the services of professional lawyers and bankers to figure out what to do. Being surrounded by experts helped her to stand her ground and not make payments on the loan. Unlike a new entrepreneur, she had the resources to weather the storm and trust her gut that the Chinese would not pursue her for loan repayment. Losing 3.5 million dollars is a big deal, no matter how successful your business is. Executives aren't immune to second-guessing their decisions, but they keep a clear and focused head, rather than panic, when monkey wrenches are thrown into the mix.

Entrepreneurial and Executive Takeaways

Paula comes to the realization that she is both manager and entrepreneur. The stereotypes of both often leave the other side with a negative connotation of their meanings. Using the skill sets inherent to each and accepting the characteristics of both gives the individual a clear sense of how to start, build, manage and grow successful businesses.

Trust is a valuable commodity to an executive and to the entrepreneur as well. Executives need to be able to have faith that the team they assemble can meet their expectations and get the job done. For entrepreneurs, it's impossible to take on every responsibility even though they best know the work involved. Trusting in others, in your product or service and in the continuing purchase power of the people who use it is a critical factor in most business decisions.

Chapter 7
First Impressions

Paula wasn't the only one facing big changes. Over the last few years at NTN, a lot of things had started to take off. We even won our very own Emmy Award. We were honored for creating a new technology in the world of television. Our additional audio track married on top of the video of old movies had grown into its very own network. We now tracked shows of all kinds including dramas, westerns, and even sitcoms. We set up a studio downstairs—a real studio, not one with boat cushions on the walls—which now basically runs twenty-four hours per day. We had state-of-the-art sound equipment, sound-proof recording rooms and experienced sound technicians and editors. Yes, this was the big time.

With things running so smoothly, my entrepreneurial bug began to come back. I think entrepreneurs are somewhat addicted to adrenaline. When a business is up and running, all the problems are solved and the processes work like clockwork, an entrepreneur starts looking for the nearest exit. We start looking for that next big idea. This is part of the reason I needed Paula. I had to control my serial impulses and really focus on managing what I had already started. She had helped me a lot, and I found myself injecting new ideas and models into NTN which helped it grow much faster than it would have on its own. But now I was getting the real itch, an itch I couldn't just wish away.

Many times entrepreneurs leave their existing, stable businesses to start something completely unrelated to their previous venture. I didn't feel right about hiring a CEO for NTN and creating a new business from scratch. I wanted to build businesses that helped build NTN and vice versa. Everything I have done since then, I have built as businesses with symbiotic relationships to each other. I knew I wanted to write; I had a lot of stories to tell, and I knew that a lot of those stories would someday make great movies. I wondered if there was a way, by building these other businesses, that each could serve as promotional tools for my core business, NTN.

I sat behind my desk thinking about my next big move. My phone was not ringing, my staff was not coming in to ask me questions, and all I could hear was the sound of a business at work. I knew it wasn't just me that needed me to find something else to do—my staff needed it too. If I stayed and kept trying to force myself into the mix, I would drive them crazy with micromanagement. They needed the next big thing as much as I did.

I made an appointment for the next day on my assistant Dorothy's schedule that ran from 8am to 5pm, and made the same appointment again the next day. I titled the appointments "Writing."

I dictated words to Dorothy that I had been up all night planning out. She typed quickly, rarely having to ask me to repeat myself. I told Dorothy a story—a parable—about a spoiled boy who had been given everything all his life from his wealthy family. When his rich uncle dies, the boy shows up expecting to receive his share of the inheritance. What he gets is very different, and at the end of the book, he is a very different person. I called the book, *The Ultimate Gift*. I knew as I was writing it that this was the book that was needed. This was a book that people would read and buy for their friends and family. This was the next big thing.

When a major publisher picked up *The Ultimate Gift*, it confirmed my suspicions. The book became very successful, a bestseller, and was later turned into a movie with James Garner and Abigail Breslin. All the while, NTN hummed in the background; we did the additional audio tracks on the DVDs for 20th Century Fox's release of *The Ultimate Gift*. This was a huge step forward for our business, and a great example that my other ventures—books, movies, TV and eventually, syndicated columns—were just adding fuel to NTN's fire of success.

My team began to work as my support staff as I had found my next passion: writing. Books poured out of me—stories, novels, business books and books about financial planning. Each project had a tie-in with NTN, which helped us gain relationships with and forge ahead into new industries.

I had come a long way from our broom closet and I had a lot to be thankful for. I thought back on those early times a lot. I considered how lucky I was to have found the few people that believed in me when they had no evidence to show them I was worth believing in: Steve Forbes, Ted Turner and of course, Paula. I thought a lot about other entrepreneurs out there who were struggling to make it, whether in a broom closet or a cubicle.

I called Dorothy in to my office, ready to type. I began just spitting out my thoughts in no organized fashion.

What is the tipping point for an entrepreneur?

Is the first impression the key to success?

As entrepreneurs, we are required to be at our very best when we are least equipped to do so…

How much of the buying decision is based on the first impression?

What is the difference between making a first impression to a potential client versus making a first impression to a new or potential employee?

I knew I needed a new perspective. I remembered getting on the phone all those years ago and being persistent about getting a yes or no answer. Looking back on that, I knew that was one way of making a first impression, and it was very effective for me. Would that work for other entrepreneurs? With several different personality types and cultural factors to be taken into consideration, I refused to think there was one approach that would work for everyone.

I made a call to Paula to see what she thought of this whole thing. I knew that being an executive, a manager and a woman would affect how she thought about the first impression.

"Hey there, Paula. How are things?" We fell into our comfortable conversation as if we had been speaking every day; in reality it had been months since we last spoke.

"Things are booming over here, Jim. But it's nothing compared to what you've got going on, Mr. Bestseller!"

"Oh stop, you're going to make me blush," I said. "But thank you, yes, I'm really enjoying the book business…"

"And the movie business, from what I hear."

"Yes, we've been very blessed—I even got to make a cameo in the movie. I play the limo driver!"

"You just go full speed ahead into everything you do. Someday I want to write a book too, but that's probably a conversation for another day, isn't it?"

"Well, that's certainly something to talk about, but it isn't why I called. As usual, instead of calling you to catch up, I'm calling you to talk about something I've been thinking about…"

"Oh, I love these calls. They give me a break from my usual meetings to talk about fun things with you."

"Well, good. I've been thinking about first impressions. As an entrepreneur, the concept fascinates me. I mean, an entrepreneur has to be at their very best when they are least equipped. How much do you think first impressions affect the buying process? What about making first impressions as an executive or as a boss? How is that different? I'm working on this for an article, I think, but maybe later on down the line it could be for a book."

"Well, that is a very interesting idea. First impressions are huge. If you think back over your life, is there anyone that had a bad first impression of you that you ended up doing business with? Probably not very many. In the sales process, I would say that first impressions are one of the most important deciding factors. However, it's very different if you are making a first impression as a boss within your company, or as a new employee to your new colleagues. I think your impression should be tweaked according to the situation."

"Well what about as a woman? Do you think being a woman has changed people's impression of you? Do you feel that, as a woman, you have to change the way you talk or present yourself?"

"I guess it's kind of hard to say because I have never been anything else! But I think yes, in the early years after I took over, I tried to conform to what was predominately a male workforce. I wore nice suits, spent hours on my hair in the morning and really just hoped that no one would call attention to the fact that I was a woman. I tried to be overly dominant in meetings and make sure my voice was heard, so I knew my team wasn't seeing me as timid or matronly. But I also asked a lot of questions and I actually listened to the answers people gave me. That was something that usually didn't happen in a male-dominated work environment. Leaders were expected to have all the answers, and their subordinates were expected to follow orders. There was almost no collaboration. So when I started incorporating people's opinions and listening to their ideas, I think that did a lot for the way I was perceived. I don't think people thought that I listened and was collaborative because I was a woman, but looking back now—after seeing many more women join the workforce—I think those traits come to be seen as inherently feminine, when they are just good practices for any team.

"As for meeting new employees versus meeting new customers, or new leads—yes, there is a very big difference because of the power dynamic. Whether it is present and talked about or not, the power dynamic is there. Being aware of it will help you know which way to play the meeting. If you are in power, i.e. if you are the boss, the other people in the meeting or gathering might be nervous about interacting with you. In that case, I think it's important to make an effort to be approachable and friendly. However, some bosses would disagree. They want to stay removed and disengaged because it makes them feel more powerful to have their employees be afraid of them. To me, this is taking two steps backward because when you need that employee to be engaged and involved with their work, you will have to first break through that fear. But on the flip side of the coin, if you are the employee, or if you are the one trying to sell something, then the power is against you. In this situation, it's important to remember what you bring to the table. You are not a beggar on the street; you have something legitimate and honest to bring to this interaction. Also, try to stay away from flagrantly fawning over the person in power—no one likes that. But I think it really comes down to personality and being true to yourself. Most seasoned business people can sense a fraud from a mile away. I have made the most important and deep business connections by just being myself."

"Well, that is all really great advice. It's a good thing I had Dorothy in here taking notes! So you think there are different approaches to making a first impression that would work for different people and different situations?"

"Yes, I do think that, and I think that some strategies would work for some people as long as they ring true with who those people really are."

"Talking to you has given me the exact idea I needed to help refine my thoughts. Thank you so much again for your wisdom and your time."

Paula gracefully ended her conversation with me and I dove right in to the ideas that had been sparking since she and I had started talking.

We think of the first impression as tragically out of our control. While there are some elements of it that *are* out of our control, much of it can be controlled. As I can see it, there are six different types of first impressions that can lead to positive results. They are:

Salesy. As this is the most common, I am listing this one first. However, I do not think it is the most effective, especially for first-time entrepreneurs. If you have a persuasive and contagious personality, then the salesy approach can work for you. The salesy approach involves being loud and dominating the conversation, always steering it back to talk about what you want to talk about. This approach tends to work better for men, but let me caution you—this approach is fading out dramatically. Younger consumers do not respond well to being sold. The stereotype of the fast-talking salesman does not conjure up good imagery most of the time. Be careful with this approach, and maybe try to pepper in some of the other approaches below.

Warm and Friendly. This approach focuses much more on relationship building and finding common ground with your counterpart. This works very well if you are the one on the positive end of the power dynamic. Making jokes and being lighthearted shows you are human and that you are open to making a new friend, and possibly business partner. This technique does not lend itself to a hard close, and you have to arrange several meetings before you "seal the deal" if this is your sales technique. Often, this technique mixes well with the "Asking Questions" technique below.

To the Point. This was always my choice, but there are reasons that I preferred "To the Point" during my early years. I was pretty insignificant in comparison to the people I was selling to. Even when I was asking people for mentorship, I found it better to be more direct. The reason is simple: time. When you are talking to people in high positions, or celebrities, or people with lots of money, you can bet they don't have a lot of time. This technique works best when paired with "Warm and Friendly." Also, when you sense a pause coming from the other end of the phone line, or from the other side of the table, take that as your cue that it's time to wrap it up.

Authoritative. This approach is best used sparingly and only when appropriate. It can be very effective in negotiating, but only when you are on the positive side of the power dynamic. I would caution against using the authoritative approach when you are trying to sell to someone or when you have just gotten hired. Authoritative people tend to lead the conversation and rarely use humor or small talk to lighten the mood.

Quiet and Listening. I want to stress that listening is never a bad idea. As Paula said in our conversation, once she began listening and collaborating with her staff, she received much different treatment, and encountered more excited team members. Listening is a highly undervalued skill that can sometimes seal the deal, even when your prospect won't be able to tell you why they liked you so much. But you have to be very careful with the quiet routine, making sure that the things you do say are well thought out and articulated. If you are a more quiet and controlled person, this approach should be easy for you. When you are meeting another person who is also naturally quiet however, be careful to avoid awkward pauses—you may have to step up your personality to compensate.

Asking Questions. This approach should always be a part of your sales strategy, but when meeting someone for the first time, it can really get the conversation going. You can implement "Asking Questions" into any other approach above, but it works best with "Warm and Friendly" and "To the Point". If you are just getting to know the person in a networking scenario, asking questions about their business and their role can help you find common ground or a possible in for your product or service. If you want to keep things more casual, asking about favorite travel locales or about someone's family will always get them talking. The goal here is to learn as much about this person as you can so that you can be a resource for them in business or in their personal life. "Asking Questions" gets you out of your head and keeps you from solely talking about yourself.

It is important to remember that although we can hone a first impression of ourselves, we cannot control every part of it. Cultural perceptions and family values help to shape people's first impressions, and there is no way to know those biases going in. You may wear your nicest suit and shine your shoes, but if the person you are meeting believes that these are symbols of corporate greed, then you are not going to make a great first impression no matter what you do.

This brings me to maybe the most important part of a first impression: knowing your audience. With so many websites at our disposal, there is no excuse for not knowing who you are meeting prior to talking with them. You should know what they do, what their position is, what their interests are, and how you can help them. When I became friends with Ted Turner, I always felt indebted to him, but what can you give Ted Turner that he doesn't already have? Well, I found out he supported the Special Olympics very heavily and I arranged to make a few appearances, since I was on the Olympic Weightlifting Team. The kids loved it, and it was really special for me to give back. I never meant for Ted to find out about it, but he did and it made our relationship stronger when he knew I would go out of my way to give something back to him, even if he wasn't actually there. Doing research on your clients and prospects is huge, and it can skip you leagues ahead in the conversation. They will be impressed you took initiative to know them, and this will lend to a positive first impression.

While researching works well for pre-planned meetings, you won't always know when opportunity is going to strike. I have met some great business connections on planes, at parties and through friends at charity events. In any of those cases, I didn't know anything about the person or their personality style. However, it's important to stay on the ball at all times, as you never know where your next lead or potential employee will come from. As Paula said, can you think back to a person you did business with who did not leave you with a good, or great, first impression? In most cases the answer is no. It's overwhelming how much the first impression potentially influences people's decisions about whether to hire you, do business with you, be friends with you or even invite you to a party. It is a topic that is often overlooked in business schools, and it's not addressed at the corporate training level. If you follow the blueprints above, nine times out of ten you will leave a great first impression

Learning Toolkit

Entrepreneurial Takeaways

Despite the fact that NTN was well managed and successful, Jim got the urge to do more. Starting a business involves having an idea, coming up with ways to make that idea more than just an idea, creating the idea, selling the idea and so on. Once the focus is solely on managing the thing that developed from that idea, entrepreneurs aren't using the skill set that is so natural to them.

Jim knew that he was better off busy than bored. He also knew that as an entrepreneur, he didn't like to be micromanaged, and shouldn't do that with his staff. He had to find the next big thing to keep his interest and his sanity intact. When the thrill begins to go, entrepreneurs best serve their businesses and themselves by coming up with new ideas to improve or expand their business.

Instead of sitting around complaining that he was bored or getting in the way of his staff, Jim came up with his next venture. He believed that his new book was the book people needed, without hesitation. This is the belief system that true entrepreneurs need to have. They are able to successfully pitch their products and ideas because they have no doubts about their ability to be successful and the public's need for their new creation.

One of the most important things an entrepreneur can do is remain true to who they are. You cannot be all things to all people. Eventually someone will see through that and won't trust you. Paula, though a seasoned executive, has made her most important and deepest business connections by being herself. Entrepreneurs can also benefit by knowing who their audience is, and adapting, not faking, their approach to accommodate the style of their audience.

Even though most entrepreneurs are all about their business, being too pushy and obsessive about it will turn people off. Good entrepreneurs know that the real emphasis is all about the consumer, not the product or service.

Entrepreneurial Takeaways continued

Entrepreneurs should make a conscious effort to pinpoint their style. Whether you are assertive, friendly, open-minded, to the point, a negotiator, a listener or one who asks a lot of questions, when you know the type of personality you are, you will know the type of impression you make on people. One essential trait of a good entrepreneur is the ability to manipulate personal style to make the audience more comfortable and accommodate their needs. Entrepreneurs should always be prepared to make a good first impression. They are the face of their company and their success depends on it.

Executive Takeaways

An executive's dream day seems to be Jim's recurring nightmare. Business was running smoothly, no questions or problems to address, money coming in, profits being made. But executives always understand that problems and situations will arise, and aren't afraid to do what needs to be done to solve them to get to their ultimate goal of a smooth, trouble-free business.

While developing a new business venture was the adrenaline rush Jim needed, he knew enough to find a way to incorporate his new ventures with his existing company. Rather than an "I'm bored, let's move on to something else" attitude, he merged his new passions with his old ones and found a pragmatic, logical way to grow his company in the process.

Paula points out that listening to her staff, asking questions, incorporating their ideas and collaborating with them are good business practices. Executives need to be strong leaders, but part of being a good leader is knowing that you don't have all the answers, but finding out where you can get them and trusting the people who work for you.

While many executives have naturally authoritative personalities, keep in mind that this instills a certain degree of fear in employees and builds a barrier between an executive and his staff. As Paula says, before an authoritative executive can get honest feedback and employee engagement, they have to first break through the fear they created. Being approachable nets far better results in terms of employee collaboration and productivity.

When Jim arranged to make a few appearances at the Special Olympics, his reasons were inspired by Ted Turner's interest in and support of them. Jim wasn't trying to make a sale—he'd already accomplished that—but rather he wanted to give back to a cause that meant something to someone who made a difference in his life. The point is, Jim did all of the research he needed to do to find out this information. The executive knows the importance of being systematic and doing exhaustive research to find out as much as there is to know about every prospect and potential client. Ignorance is simply no excuse for lack of information.

Chapter 8
Cash is King, Credit is God

It had been too long, simply too long, since Jim and I had seen each other face to face. I felt that all our conversations were harried, which was the nature of our lives at the time, but that was no excuse. We had made a pact that we would be there for each other and support each other, not just as mentors, but as friends. I liked to say we were "friendtors," as neither of us was the mentor or the mentee; our roles flexed between both depending on the topics we were discussing. It was a delicate balance, but I wasn't about to go one more minute without setting up a breakfast.

When we both found a time that would work, I packed up my car with a few presents for Jim. I had been traveling a lot and had collected little tokens from across the globe that I thought he would like. Of course, packing the gifts and remembering everything made me a little late, but I knew Jim would probably expect that. When I walked into the restaurant, there he was, waiting on me. My arms were full of trinkets, but I did my best to hug him anyway.

"It has just been so long, Jim," I said. "I brought you some gifts to make up for all the time!"

When I said Jim's name I felt many of the restaurant's eyes on us. Jim had become much more well known from the man I met years ago, and the prying eyes knew something big must be happening. I doled out my gifts and we laughed and caught up.

"So you've been traveling so much, have you found your favorite country yet?" Jim asked.

"It's so hard to have a favorite, since they're all so different, but you know, I really just love the good old U.S. of A."

"I agree with you, it is hard to compare. I've been speaking more, and we're about to organize a big speaking tour. We'll be traveling to a lot of countries I've never been to, so that's exciting."

"Speaking? Like motivational speaking?"

"Exactly that. Companies have started bringing me in as a speaker to motivate their people. It's a lot of fun. The biggest one I've done so far was for about 20,000 people in Vegas. It's great, I just tell them my story and they clap. I can't think of anything I'd rather do than just talk to people, and this way, I get to talk to thousands and hopefully help them see something about themselves they didn't see before."

I sat in admiration for a moment. "Jim, that is amazing. I really think that is something I would like to do someday. You'll have to go ahead and report back to me from the front lines. I am just getting teary-eyed thinking about all those people's lives you're touching!"

"Yeah, it's pretty great…"

Just then someone approached our table. I was so engrossed in what Jim was saying that I didn't look up. But Jim sensed the person and turned in their direction. I looked toward my menu, thinking it must be time to order my meal.

"E-excuse me, Mr. Stovall… Mrs. Marshall… ugh, I can't believe I'm doing this, just interrupting you like this. You see, I recognized Mr. Stovall from his book cover, and you, Mrs. Marshall—I've seen you in the paper. I know you do a lot of work with the Chamber of Commerce. I… I was just wondering if you had a few moments, because… I'm an entrepreneur."

I could see that the man was young, maybe in his late twenties. He was dressed in jeans and a long-sleeved button-up shirt; he was obviously not expecting to have this conversation today. I could tell he was nervous, and after talking about changing people's lives with public speaking it felt wrong to just turn him away. But since Jim was technically the entrepreneur of the two of us, I was prepared to let him take the lead.

"Well, I think we can spare a few minutes. Here, you should take a seat— what's your name, son?" Jim was composed, as if this happened to him all the time. And then I realized that it probably did. People must approach him all the time after his speeches and ask for his advice.

"My name's Ken, Ken Richards. I... I... can't thank you enough for talking to me. I know it's so rude to interrupt your meal, but I saw the two of you together and I just couldn't miss a chance like this. Mrs. Marshall, I've followed your career and the success of Bama Pie my whole life. My family lived over near 11th street, and we would pass your plant every day on the way to school."

"Well, thank you. If you're an entrepreneur you've come to the right table— this man is who you want to talk to," I said, gesturing at Jim.

"What's your business, Ken?" Jim asked.

"I... well, I say I'm an entrepreneur, but what I really mean is I want to be one. Right now I work for Williams Companies, but it's not my passion. I've been there since I left college, but I've had this business idea in the back of my head for a few years. It just kept growing and growing and now it's almost all I can think about. I don't think I can go my whole life without at least trying it." Ken lit up when he began to speak about becoming an entrepreneur.

"Well, don't keep us in suspense. What's your idea?" I could tell Jim was genuinely excited. He was born to do this.

"In my spare time, I love to cycle. I cycle long distances and have a group of friends I ride with. A few times per week we go out on long rides, sometimes up to 60 miles. I want to open a cycling store—sell bikes, bike equipment, attire, water bottles, and even fix bikes and give them tune-ups. The cycling world is growing, and it's really my true passion. I've drawn store layouts again and again, I have inventory sheets made up, I've researched and talked to suppliers..."

"Ken," Jim cut him off, "did you sit down here today so I could tell you that you have a great idea, maybe even offer to be an investor, or did you sit down here so that you could really learn something and possibly have a great business one day?"

Jim's reaction took me by surprise, even though I was wondering the same thing.

"Sir...?"

"What I'm saying, Ken, is that there is what you need to know, and what you want to know—those are two different answers. Do you want me to tell you what you *need* to know, or just pat you on the back and tell you that you have a great idea?"

Ken sat silent for a moment, really considering the question. Jim waited patiently. "I want to know what you know. Asking you for money or for praise isn't going to get me anywhere. I want to know what I need to know to make this happen."

"Well, that's the answer I hoped you'd choose, but you may not like what I have to say. I do like your idea, but the success of retail depends a lot on location and reputation. A retail store is very expensive to start—how are you going to get the money?"

"I'm preparing my executive summary and I'm going to set up a meeting at my bank. I think I have a decent chance of getting a small business loan," Ken said. Jim sat stone-faced, but I had to look away for a moment so that I didn't give away what I was thinking.

"Well, the first advice I can give you is this: banks will only give you money when you don't need it. Almost no bank will give an entrepreneur starting out a loan. If they did, there would be so many new ventures all the time we wouldn't be able to keep up. The bank wants to know beyond a shadow of a doubt that you will be able to pay them back, even if you go out of business. The only way they can know that is if you already have the money.

"Let me tell you, the place you need to look for money is your Christmas card list. Your family and friends. I know everybody says that you shouldn't borrow money from family, but that is the best bet for something like this. If it makes you feel more comfortable, go to a lawyer and have them draw up loan documents, just as if they were a bank. You can even pay interest if you think potential lenders would be more comfortable with that arrangement. You've got to have your numbers drawn out exactly where you want them, down to the last line item. Which brings me to my next question: how much do you make at Williams?"

"Uh…well, my base pay is $50,000, and then there are benefits…"

"How are you going to get paid while the business is growing? Do you have any savings?"

"Well, I have a mortgage and a few other bills, but I think I could live on $45,000 with no benefits for a few months, but then the business will pay me, right?" Ken looked hopeful.

"No, Ken; you shouldn't take a salary until your business is making a profit. That means until all the loans are paid back and you are guaranteed earnings beyond your breakeven point. Some people build a salary into their loan, but they keep it very low; you see, you can't eat your seed corn.

"Cash is king, especially in an inventory-based business. A lot of your value will be tied up in inventory, so if you want to make any decisions, you've got to have some cash on hand to play with. I would count on three years of time, so add up how much money you need to survive for three years, and start stockpiling that. If you aren't able to pay yourself after three years, you need to reconsider your business plan."

"Wow, I just hadn't thought about it like that. It could take years for me just to save up all that money…"

I saw this young man's dreams crashing down around him. But everything Jim had said was true. It was the early 2000s and people were just beginning to understand the power of the internet. I didn't know much about it at the time, but I wanted to offer my two cents.

"Ken, I know this information comes as a shock, but everything Jim is telling you is true. What I always tell young people who want to do startups is to start small. Maybe you could just start with an online store, have a small inventory and then grow from there. Once you have a running online business with some money coming in, you could use that to support you when you open your brick and mortar store. You can start and run your online store while keeping your job at Williams. That way the money from the online store can go directly into your 'Brick and Mortar Store Savings Fund.'"

"That could work, I guess. I just don't know much about the internet or online stores…"

"Well, really, how much do you know about running a brick and mortar store?" Jim asked. "From what you've told us, not much. You would be learning as you go either way. I always see this with young entrepreneurs—you guys get starry-eyed about the details. For you it's how your store is going to look, the name of the store, the cool things your store will have… for a restaurateur it's the same. They love to dream about the menus and the salt and pepper shakers. These things are important to a business, of course, but not until you have the funding.

"Don't get caught up in the excitement of owning a cycling shop, at least not until you're sure you can make it a reality. It's like looking at houses: you look and look for a house that's perfect for you and your family. The realtor takes you to one house in the perfect neighborhood, with marble counter tops, a study for you and even extra bedrooms. As soon as you walk in, you can see yourself lounging in an armchair by the fireplace. You can see your kids playing in the back yard. You can smell dinner cooking in the kitchen. Suddenly, you must have it. You ignore the budget you set for yourself, and you buy the bigger house with all the trimmings because clearly it was meant for you. Before you know it you're drowning in debt and bills and you ask yourself how you got here. This is what you're doing with your business. You'll be drowning before you even have a chance to succeed."

"I have to admit, Mr. Stovall, when you asked me if I wanted to hear this, I was sure I did… but now, I'm not so sure. I mean, you're right. The dream is the glamorous part. Thinking about creating a community of cyclists and being the guy who was able to take the first step, that is very romantic to me. But the money situation… I always just thought it would work itself out if I followed my dream."

"Ken, if that were true, there would be no failed businesses. It's great to have a dream and I count myself blessed every day that I have been able to follow mine, but it wasn't easy. When I first started my business, people just thought I got to work really early and that I was the last to leave. Well, the truth was—I was sleeping there. I had nowhere else to go. Every sale looked like a bag of groceries. I was able to manage the business to a sustainable level partly because I was very careful with the money we had. You need startup money to get you through the rough times when you aren't getting paid, bills are coming in, and you aren't making any sales. You can't expect to go in the first day and just start selling everything like hot cakes. Building a business takes time, and that's why cash is king—because it buys you time."

Ken sat quietly. He knew what Jim was saying was the truth, but he didn't want to believe it. He was still holding on to the romance of owning a business.

"Ken," I said, "think about your options. Think about opening an online store first and compare those costs with a real store. See what you can make work. Right now it seems hopeless, but if your dream is going to become a reality, you have to be strong enough to weather the tough times. If your dream truly is bigger than you, and you think it should happen no matter what, even if you have nothing to do with it, there will be a way."

"Well, I really want to thank you for your time and expertise. I'm sorry again for interrupting your meal." Ken seemed as deflated as a week-old helium balloon.

"Thanks for coming over to talk to us; that took a lot of courage. I think you'll do well in the bike business."

Jim had just given this young man some serious things to think about, but that last comment, "I think you'll do well in the bike business," showed that Jim still believed in Ken despite his no-nonsense advice. Even though Jim had just met Ken, he wanted to leave him with some hope for the future.

Ken straightened tall as he walked away from the table. Jim's last comment had had the intended effect. Entrepreneurs weather a lot of blows in the first few years in business, and most of them do not have the education that Jim had just bestowed upon Ken. But if he could take the advice and still build a business, he would prove himself a true entrepreneur.

"Jim, did I ever tell you the story of how my grandfather, Henry Marshall, got the financing to start Bama?" I knew Jim would get a kick out of this little piece of history.

"No. It sounds like one that would be appropriate to the subject matter," Jim said with a chuckle.

"Well, my grandmother Alabama, who's the namesake for our company—Bama being one of her nicknames, the other being Big Mother—was working at the Woolworth's Drug Store making pies. They had a soda jerk station and served lunch daily, but the news of the town became the pies. People could not get enough. So my grandfather, Henry, saw an opportunity. He asked my grandmother, 'Why should Mr. Woolworth get all the money from all those pies you're sellin', when he's just paying you hourly? Let's start our own business makin' those pies of yours.'

"And so they did just that. But they needed an inventory to start baking, and this was in Texas during the Great Depression. He told Big Mother he needed all their money for supplies. She wearily reached into the money jar and pulled out all they had left—$1.67. He went up to the Charles Dennery Bakery Supply and introduced himself to the man behind the counter as Mr. H.C. Marshall, owner of the Bama Pie Company. 'Because of your company's high standards and impeccable reputation, I've chosen to purchase my supplies from you.'

"The shop manager just beamed. He took out his order forms and a pencil as Big Dad started spouting off ingredients. 'Four pounds of cherries, fifteen pounds of apples, four pounds of pineapples, five pounds each of dried peaches and apples, two twelve-quart enamel pans, two dozen seven-inch pie pans and one pound each of salt and cinnamon.'

"The stock boy began filling the truck with all the things Big Dad requested and the store manager added up everything. 'That'll be twenty-five dollars and fifty cents, Mr. Marshall.' Big Dad didn't even flinch. Matter-of-factly he said, 'I have one dollar and sixty-seven cents to pay down on the supplies and I promise, by my word, I will pay you the balance in thirty days.' The store manager sat speechless. All he managed to say was, 'What?' When Big Dad repeated himself, the store manager answered him with silence. The stock boy came in to say that the truck had been loaded. I don't know if it's because he didn't want to have his employee unload the car, or because he trusted Big Dad's word, but the manager agreed to the terms and they shook hands. That's how we got into the pie business. And Big Dad did pay him back every cent of that first order, plus many more orders to come after that. I think my grandfather was the original example of bootstrapping your business!"

"That is an amazing story, and that's exactly what entrepreneurs have to do. I don't recommend starting a business with no money, but more often than not that is what we have to do. It's not glamorous, and it's not pretty, but it sure is fun. I miss those days sometimes—but then I remember that I like to eat!" We were both laughing now, and we finished the remainder of our meal as friends who hadn't seen each other in a long time.

Learning Toolkit

Entrepreneurial Takeaways

Recognizing young Ken's eagerness about opening his own business, Jim offered to tell him the brutal truth about starting out as an entrepreneur. Based on his own experience, he knew that he could help Ken understand the reality of what he hoped to accomplish. Though his words may have seemed discouraging, Jim believed it was better to be honest. Succeeding as an entrepreneur is no easy feat; it was kind of Jim to pass along his hard-earned knowledge to help a prospective business owner find his way. Before taking the leap into opening your own business, seek out a trusted entrepreneur who is willing to give you the honest truth about the road you're about to travel.

Jim's advice that Ken skip the bank and approach family and friends for a business loan would most likely save the young man considerable time. With his experience, Jim knew that banks would want collateral and a repayment schedule that might be impossible for Ken to maintain during his start-up phase. If you decide to ask people you know to lend you money or to invest in your business, be professional. Explain your business plan, have your facts and figures ready, and be prepared to sign documents ensuring that you will repay all loans.

Like all entrepreneurs, Ken wanted to open his business to pursue his passion and to make money. He did not realize that taking a salary would be nearly impossible until he had repaid his loans and was making more money than he needed in order to break even. As Jim advised, be prepared to have three years' worth of capital saved up in order to maintain your living expenses. If you are still unable to draw a salary after three years, you should revisit your business plan and make some adjustments. That might be another good time to ask an established entrepreneur for some advice.

After hearing advice from two pros, Ken acknowledged that he had been romanticizing the idea of opening his business to the point of avoiding the realities of what would be needed to make it work. Without his chance encounter with Jim and Paula, Ken might have moved forward with his venture before he was able to make it a success. Don't wait for chance or coincidence to determine your future. If starting a business is your dream, learn exactly what you need to know and take the necessary steps to plan accordingly. A delayed dream that succeeds is far better than an impulsive one that fails.

Entrepreneurial Takeaways continued

Narrative Television Network's success was due to Jim's commitment to working extremely hard in the early days of the company. As he told Ken, every sale represented his next meal. Be prepared to work long hours, possibly doing several jobs at once if you aren't able to hire employees. Be very careful with the money you have in order to stay current with vendors and creditors. Most of all, be patient. It takes time for a business to build a reputation, but your hard work and belief in your talents will serve you well if you are willing to put in the time to build a successful business.

Following Paula's advice may be a sound option for many entrepreneurs. Particularly if your business idea is to open a retail store, starting with an online store could allow you to keep your current job and accumulate additional capital while the business gets up and running. Tweaking your plans a bit might allow you to start sooner than you'd expected and still earn enough money to live on while the business grows.

Executive Takeaways

Paula refers to herself and Jim as "friendtors." Even though she is a very successful executive in her own right, she knows the value of having an advisor to whom she can turn for counsel and support. It's important for executives to spend time with trusted colleagues; this can not only enhance their business productivity but can also add a welcome freshness to their overall approach to work and life. While Paula and Jim do discuss business, they do so in a less formal setting that lets them both relax.

Paula's suggestion that Ken start his business online is sound advice from her executive perspective. She knows the cost and time that go into getting a business off the ground and can offer this guidance based on her grandparents' decision to start a small pie business that led to the incredible success of Bama. It's great to dream big, but it's equally important to start with a manageable operation that can grow from the ground up.

Chapter 9
Bagging the Elephant

I had begun to sit on several advisory boards for small companies that were just starting out. First it began as a favor to a friend, then more and more business owners began to approach me via email to ask if I would sit on their boards. It was and is something I really enjoy doing. I can help entrepreneurs and small businesses avoid some of the mistakes that are common when businesses are growing.

Some people would purport that starting a business is the hard part, but I maintain that *growing* a business is the hard part. At NTN, where we had very little startup capital, it was hard to get to a place where I felt comfortable spending any money. When there's no money to spend, that's easy, you don't buy anything. But when you start to pick up momentum and there is a little cash in the bank, that's when hard decisions have to be made. What to buy, how much to buy and how much money to keep in reserves—those are the decisions that will make or break a business. That point between being a small business and a medium business can depend on a lot of factors, and most of those factors have to do with who your customers are and how you spend your money.

One day I was sitting in a board meeting for a company owned by a friend of mine. The company's primary business is making signs—For Sale signs, Garage Sale signs, that kind of thing. They are signs you would also be able to buy in a mega-chain store like Wal-Mart or Home Depot. At this point in their business, my friend's company was distributing to small hardware stores and regional grocery chains. The owner ha' his sights set on becoming the main supplier to Home Depot. It had been his dream since the company had legs to stand on.

"Jim, I just got word that Home Depot is looking for a new supplier for their signs." John, my friend and the owner of the company, could barely contain his excitement. He saw this opening as a sign—excuse the pun—that he was meant to fulfill his dream. The other members of the board started shaking hands and congratulating John on this new and exciting opportunity. I listened to them all, buzzing with potential and excitement. I wanted to join in, but it was my duty on this board to advise the company, and I didn't feel it was right to jump into a celebration without really thinking the decision through. This decision could change the whole landscape of their business—sure, it could be in a good way, but it could also be detrimental to their operations and cause major financial upheaval.

"Guys, let's think about this. John, I know this has been something you've wanted for a long time. But you've got to think about how this is going to impact your business. Going after this contract could be a bad idea..." My words were followed by silence.

"Jim, are you crazy? This is it! We've made it! We'll be rolling in profits by the time the year is out. What do you mean, bad idea? If you think making millions of dollars is a bad idea..." The rest of the board made sounds of agreement and laughter.

"Listen, I've been your friend for a long time. Just do me the favor of meeting with someone. I have a friend whose company supplies to a major chain—in fact, the biggest chain there is. I want you to come with me to meet her. I just want you to understand both sides of the story—dealing with these chains is not all dollar signs."

"Jim, the Request for Proposal is due by the end of this month. If we're going to submit something, we have to start now. I don't have time to wait for a meeting."

"Well, start getting your ducks in a row for the proposal, and I will see what I can do. If she knows it's important, she'll meet with us on short notice." I hoped Paula wasn't halfway across the world.

"Jim, what about you? You work with NBC, Fox, and other huge conglomerates. How can you say it's not all about the dollar signs?"

"Yes, we have done well working with big companies, but that is not the case for everyone. If you get too enamored with the idea, you will let them walk ꞏll over you, all for the glory of saying you supply to Home Depot. There are some things you need to know about dealing with these chains and I think my friend Paula can help shed some light on the subject. Will you just come with me to meet with her?"

"Okay, but don't expect me to change my mind."

"I don't expect anything from you, except that you listen with an open mind," I said. I knew John was stubborn, and that he would probably go after the contract no matter what anyone said to him. But he asked me to be on his advisory board, and I take that role very seriously. At least he would not be able to say that he didn't go into this deal with his eyes open.

~~~~~

Luckily, Paula was available to meet with us within the week. We sat down for bagels and coffee in, ironically, a large restaurant chain. John was annoyed that I had made him come to the meeting in the first place.

"Jim, what do you expect this is going to accomplish? You and Paula are not going to talk me out of the biggest business deal of my life."

"I don't expect to talk you out of it. I suspect at the end of our talk you will be even more excited to go after the deal than ever. To talk you out of it is not the point of this meeting. The point of this meeting is to make sure you are fully aware and informed about the reality of working with a mega-chain. It is not as simple as just submitting the proposal and getting the job. There are other factors that will impact your business in the long run, and these are things you need to be thinking about instead of getting distracted by the dollars." John didn't respond but I could feel his reluctance.

"Hey guys! Did everyone get coffee? And bagels? I just ordered and I got some extras just in case." Paula had arrived just in time it seemed. "Hi, is it John? I'm Paula Marshall."

"Hi Paula, it's really a pleasure to meet you. I've heard so much about your work in the community and the work you do at Bama," John said. He was ready to turn on the charm now that Paula was actually there.

"Well thank you, John. Jim tells me you've got a big opportunity for your company on the horizon?"

"Yes, we are a sign company—the kind of signs you see in people's yards. Home Depot just announced they're looking for a new supplier and it's always been my dream to supply to a national chain…"

"Talk to me about that—why is that your dream? What does supplying to a national chain mean to you?" Paula asked.

"It means success. It means I can take my kids into the store and say, 'Look, Daddy makes those signs.' It means I've made it. We've been profitable for the past few years supplying to regional chains and mom-and-pop stores, but I want more. Supplying to a national chain means I won't ever have to worry about money again. My kids' colleges will be paid for, my employees can get raises… it means I've done it. I've beaten the odds."

"Well, I think the reason Jim wanted me to talk to you was to talk about my experience with large chains, and particularly my most recent customer. They are the largest chain retail store in the world. In the last two years we've started supplying frozen biscuits to them. However, I have to tell you, when we got that customer, we were already prepped and primed for a large-scale operation. We had bargaining power—we are one of the only companies equipped to produce biscuits on the scale they needed. Because of this we were able to negotiate and still have some footing.

"If you are going into this knowing that Home Depot will be your first large-scale client, then you will have to prove to them that you will build the facilities they need and meet their quotas. That doesn't put you in a good place for negotiating. And they know that. The first place they will hit you will be the price—they'll want to pay less than any of your other customers. Probably half the price. And you'll be competing with products that are made overseas for a fraction of the cost. They will use all of these things as bargaining chips to get you to lower your price. When you factor in the investment it will take to build out your manufacturing operation to their specs, you will be in the hole a lot of money."

"Yes, but the long term profits will pay for the changes to the machinery and all that…" John was beginning to sound unsure.

"Well that could be true, but they will want you to fix the price on your product for the remainder of your contract. That means that even if the price of materials goes up, you will be getting the same amount for your product. And if they don't like it, they will just get another company, like they're doing now."

"John, the risk you're taking is this," I said. "I have seen several companies do business with these large chains and three things happen. You commit the majority of your manufacturing time to this one order, these companies are notoriously slow to pay, and they've squeezed you down to where you're making pennies on each unit. Once you combine all those factors, it really can put you out of business. You'll have to pay suppliers for materials you haven't been paid for yet. You can grow right out of business if you don't have the money in the bank and the equipment you need."

Paula chimed in. "Another thing, and this is true with all chains, is they have a lot of cost barriers for each step of the process. They charge fees to stock the product, fees to display the product, fees to have your product in the catalog, fees to have your product up online, and on and on it goes. This is how they make their money."

"But Paula, you've built your company off of working with large chains. I think Bama is doing very well. How can you say it's all bad?" John said.

"I'm not saying it's all bad. But there is a big difference between Bama working with a chain and a small company taking a contract with Home Depot. Bama was equipped to take on such a large client. We have our lawyers and managers to represent us in a big deal like this and make sure we are creating a contract that is mutually beneficial for us and for the customer. All I'm saying is, it's important to weight the pros and cons in a deal like this, and not get caught up in the potential monetary reward." Paula was saying all the things I had hoped she would, but I didn't want John to feel we'd totally rained on his parade.

"John, you know I was a small company when I started working with the larger networks. It was a big decision for me to get into that arena. It's like that old saying, 'don't put all your eggs in one basket.' Well, I started putting jumbo eggs into my tiny basket. It has worked out well for us, but it changed the landscape of my business forever. I just wanted you to be aware that doing business with these guys is not always good. So many companies jump into it without figuring out the right agreement, and they drown. I don't want to see that happen to you. Don't get stomped by the elephant."

"So how can I avoid it? How can I go after this contract without getting crushed?"

"Well," Paula began, "there are some things you can do. You need to maintain power and pride in what you can deliver. These big companies will make you feel as if you are small time and that they don't need you. The truth is they don't need you, but they do need your product. Maintain that you are worthy, and that you don't need them to be successful. If you act as though you need their business to survive, they will smell your desperation and use it as a way to manipulate you.

"Next, it's important that you don't bend over backwards to get the deal. If you go into the meeting saying you can make X number of signs per day, and they say they need four times that, then it's not a good fit. Don't just jump and say, 'Oh, we could up our production four times...' That will hurt you when it comes time to actually do that, and you can't.

"Another important thing to remember is, your existing customers have believed in you from the beginning, and they have gotten you to a point where someone like Home Depot is interested. Many times when companies get a huge client, their customer service for the rest of their customers goes downhill. This will cause a lot of problems. If anything, you should treat your existing customers with even more reverence than before. If your huge client decides to go elsewhere, you have maintained those relationships and can survive.

"Something that we strive for at Bama is to not sacrifice quality for quantity. Now that is a very hard thing to do when you are pushing out millions of pounds of product every hour. But we take it very seriously because if something goes wrong with our customer relationships, we can always sell our quality. I mean, Home Depot isn't the only outlet that sells these kinds of signs. If this doesn't work out, you want to be able to bid on more contracts and eventually get a lot of big clients, but the only way to do that is if you have a quality product to sell. When you are focusing on ramping up your production, a lot of times quality falls by the wayside. But you can't let that happen.

"The next thing to remember is that you are going into this relationship as a partner, not a peon. The relationship has to be win-win on both sides for this to be a good fit. If they can squeeze you down on your price, they will. But you have to remind them that this is a partnership, that you have their best interests at heart and you hope they are considering your best interests too. These companies don't want to work with a supplier that is hanging on by a thread. It threatens their business and their ability to give their customers what they want. They want a stable, smart, capable company that is going to be able to go into business with them for a long time. So, when you cast yourself as their equal and say, 'here is what we're willing and able to do for you, here are the reasons you should use our company, and if we can't come to an agreement, then we'll catch you on the flip side,' it shows you are stable and confident. These are traits they are looking for in a partner.

"Okay. Those are all important, but this is the most important thing to remember when dealing with huge clients: *factor in all of your costs*. That may sound obvious, but it is a huge potential pitfall. There are hidden costs all over these big contracts and, if you are going to need to expand your production capabilities, you will need to factor in construction costs, bank loans, interest, new equipment—all of that can be enough to put you under before you even start working on those orders. If you approach them as a partner, and you are honest about what you will need, how long it will take and how much money it's going to cost you, you won't have to go back later and explain what's taking so long. Ask them about their payment procedures—how long will it take to get paid on invoices? Also, ask them about additional fees for coupon placement, catalog placement and things like that. You want to go into this with your eyes wide open."

"Paula. I think we might have scared the living daylights out of John," I said, looking at my shell-shocked friend.

"Well, from what you all have told me, I should be scared! But I am really grateful for this reality check. I was just going to go in there and tell them whatever it took to get the contract. I think that could have really put me out of business. Jim, I owe you one."

"But John, we didn't mean to talk you out of going for the contract. We just wanted you to be informed about the pros and cons. I think you guys really could end up selling to Home Depot."

"Well, I don't know. I realize now that there are a lot of internal issues that need to be addressed before we go after a company like that. I don't know if we can straighten everything out before the due date. But there will be other contracts and other opportunities in the future." John seemed a different person than when we arrived at the meeting.

"You certainly have changed your tune, John. I'm glad I could help. I think you should make it one of your company's five-year goals to land a contract with a national retailer, and keep us posted with how things go." I was glad that John saw some of the problems I had seen with his plan, and that he wasn't going to jump into something without thinking it through. John left in a hurry. It seemed he couldn't wait to get back to the office to implement some of the new ideas he'd gotten from our conversation.

I thanked Paula again for her advice and her ability to meet with us on such short notice.

"Any time, Jim. I'm glad I could help. I think it's hard when you are an entrepreneur and you see that one big contract as the end to all your troubles. I mean, my dad did exactly what we've just told John not to do. He took a right turn instead of a left turn and headed up to ask McDonald's if they wanted a dessert. But they were smaller then, and they worked with him for five years on developing the product they ended up launching. Times were so different then. Ray Kroc decided to do business with my father based on a handshake and a firm look in the eye. Companies today, these large chains, are much different now. They have 'take no prisoners' business models."

"That's exactly right. I advised a company that was not much different from John's in size and they got a contract with one of your customers—the largest retailer in the world. This contract was so ridiculous—they had them over a barrel. The company I was advising had no chance. They ended up going under within a year. I just couldn't stand by and watch that happen again."

"I hate to see that happen to entrepreneurs, especially those that mean well and work hard. I think many times, if we are strategic about who we sell to, we don't need to put ourselves in situations where we can be taken advantage of.

For example, if John chose, he could make a very good living selling to regional chains and local stores. He could build up his business and reputation on quality, and perhaps when the time was right, he could have been in position for a big contract. But he would have the choice if he wanted to work with them or not."

"Exactly. That's why I knew I could bring him to you and you would talk some sense into him!" I said with a laugh.

Paula and I said our goodbyes and went our separate ways. I was relieved we had been able to help John out of a potentially bad situation.

Learning Toolkit

Entrepreneurial Takeaways

Jim understands that while starting a business can certainly be difficult, *growing* a business is the truly hard part. Once the business begins to take off, it's important to use resources wisely and to carefully evaluate every expense to be sure that you don't run through your funds too quickly. Deciding how to spend your hard-earned money is a critical factor in staying afloat.

John was elated by his offer to submit a proposal to become a supplier to Home Depot. He saw this as proof that he had arrived, as a lock on his financial security, and was ready to jump right in before Jim advised him to slow down and consider every angle of the deal. As exciting as a big prospect may be, don't rush into anything. Take the deal apart and examine every piece before committing to something that might not be as great for your business as it initially seems.

Like many entrepreneurs, John was excited by the idea of landing his first big client, but was unable to clearly see the big picture. Paula advised him on the financial realities, which included building manufacturing facilities, negotiating product prices, and competing with overseas products, all of which would end up costing more than the contract was worth. Before entering into a large-scale deal, do a full analysis of every item that will cost you money. Also consider whether you will be required to fix the price of your products for the duration of the contract; if you can't raise your prices, you might lose money.

Jim acknowledges that while working with the networks was the right decision for NTN, it also changed his business completely. When you are considering a big business deal, think about all the ways it will affect your company, not just financially. How will your hours be impacted, will you need more staff, will your company's culture change? These are all valid, and vital, questions that require your attention. Follow Jim's advice: Don't get stomped by the elephant.

Avoid appearing desperate when negotiating with big clients; they will sense it and use it against you. Don't promise more than you can deliver or you'll be obligated to meet impossible demands.

As exciting as a big contract is, remember that it's your earlier clients who got you to this bargaining position. Never undervalue your existing clients; maintain excellent customer service across the board.

Executive Takeaways

Paula points out that when Bama began supplying products to McDonald's, they were already an established corporation with existing manufacturing facilities and the legal support they needed to ensure their position with the client. Don't enter into a deal that will require you to spend huge sums of money just to meet the requirements of the contract; this will leave you with little room for negotiation.

Even established companies can fall prey to poor decisions. If you are responsible for negotiating a big deal, be sure that your research is thorough and that the contract will benefit your company. Get input from all appropriate departments and carefully consider all aspects before making a commitment.

Paula points out that Bama does not sacrifice quality for quantity. Even when producing millions of pounds of product an hour, the company's priority is to ensure the highest quality of each item. Even a company as secure as Bama would face competition if their quality fell below customer expectations. Maintaining the highest quality is of utmost importance for every executive.

Chapter 10
Omnipreneurship

Bama had grown to the point where I didn't need to travel all the time to make deals and oversee new production. Where I was needed most was at home. Everyone knew I was the CEO, Chief Executive Officer, but I adopted a new acronym as well—CCO, or Chief Culture Officer. The acronym was self-applied, of course, but it put a focus on something that I think is very important in any organization. A great company culture does not just happen. It must be fostered. Bama was at a point in its life-cycle where it was apparent that the culture I had worked so hard to create was being threatened. I had been CEO for almost twenty years, and the principles that I put in place in the early 90s were becoming stale to the new workforce. Gen Xers had come in to replace many Baby Boomers who were retiring, and they didn't "get" many of the values I found central to Bama's culture. I began to spend more and more time on the home front so that I could play the culture doctor.

I had set up a meeting with a young man we had just hired in our IT department. To be honest, I was frustrated with my new, younger workforce, and I felt I could better understand them by speaking with Ethan. I wanted him to serve as an ambassador for younger workers, so he could teach me what I was missing. There seemed nothing I could do to motivate these Gen Xers, who did the bare minimum, couldn't wait for the weekend, and seemed completely disengaged from their work. My mission at Bama is to give people a workplace where they feel supported and loved—where they love to come to work—and it seemed there was nothing I could do to motivate my younger workers. I knew my talk with Ethan would help.

"Ethan, hi! Come in and sit down. I've been looking forward to our talk all day." I wanted to set him at ease, since usually meeting with the CEO isn't a good thing.

"Hi, Ms. Marshall. I hope I'm not here because I've done something wrong?" Ethan was about thirty. He was always professional and very technically skilled, which made him a great asset to our IT team. Though he was always at work on time, I could tell that most days there was someplace he would rather be.

"No, no Ethan. I just wanted to talk to you, to get to know you better. We have brought on so many new faces lately that I feel like I don't know anyone anymore! I just wanted to sit you down and find out what makes you tick. Let me explain a little more. I'm focusing a lot of my time right now on building Bama's culture. I feel like in the last few years it has failed to be what I want it to be, and this is something that's very important to me. I want to make sure that you, and other newer team members, have the chance to let me know what you want in a company culture. Does that make sense?"

"Yes, of course. I've never worked anywhere that actually wanted my opinion on anything like this," he said.

"Well, that's part of what I'm trying to maintain! So I want to start with you. What do you like to do outside of work?"

"Actually, I'm in a band. I love to play locally, but I also promote local shows—like I bring in bigger bands and set them up to play with a few local bands, I find the venue and then I promote the show to local media. We have a big show coming up in a couple of weeks that my band is playing."

"Oh, so do you make any money doing that, the promotion part?"

"Well, not really. It depends on how many tickets we sell. I've had a few shows that made money, but that's not why I do it. I do it because I love it."

Ethan had begun to light up, and I could tell right away that this was his true passion in life. "I also own a few rental houses. I enjoy real estate a lot. I like fixing up old houses and the whole investment aspect of it."

"So if you had to rank your interests—working in technology, real estate investing, and music—how would they stack up?"

"Well, if I'm ranking them by love, then music, technology, real estate. But if I rank them by how much money each makes, then it would be technology, real estate and music."

"Okay, so you do have a passion for IT, but if you could do anything and money was no object, you would pursue your musical career?"

"Yes, I guess that's true. But I think everyone has that one thing they would do if money were no object. If we all did those things there would be a world full of artists, musicians and couch potatoes. That's why I do something that I love to make money, but I also have other things I love to do on the side. I also think that money taints music and art to a certain extent, which is why I would rather keep them separate."

"Have you ever thought about any ways that you could incorporate your love of music into your job here at Bama? I'm asking because I want this to be a job that you love. If you're doing what you love, you're more likely to show up, do a great job, and possibly even see a better way of doing things. Innovating and constantly improving, that is the key to a successful business. I want every employee to be constantly looking for ways to improve Bama, and that means ways to constantly improve themselves too."

"Hmm… that's a really great way of bringing everything together. I noticed you have company parties every once in awhile, Bama Family Fun Day and stuff like that. I could bring my DJ equipment and DJ some of those events. I think that would be fun and it would be a good way for me to bring my music into my work here."

"Wow, what a great idea! I will make sure we get that set up for you. You have really inspired me to think differently about some of these things. I have been working so hard at Bama over the last two decades that it never occurred to me that I could do anything else with my time. But if I wanted to draw or sing or anything like that, I could and it would not affect my performance. Thank you for talking with me so candidly about this."

After my conversation with Ethan, I started thinking about ways that my employees could be more fulfilled, while still fulfilling all of their duties at work.

Naturally there are some jobs that don't lend themselves to being inspired. For example, we have a lot of people working on the manufacturing line. They pack products into boxes, get things ready to ship, and make sure the line is running at full capacity. For these folks, and folks like them, I wondered if there was a way they could follow their dreams while still doing their jobs well. I wondered if there was a way for me, as a CEO, to truly follow my dreams to be a motivational speaker while still being the best CEO I could be. I knew just the person to ask.

"Jim! It's another one of those impromptu phone calls. I hope I'm not interrupting anything?"

"No, of course not, I love our calls. What's on your mind today?"

"Well, I've been talking to some of my employees and thinking about some things. I truly believe that you have to have passion for what you do. But what if what you do isn't your passion, but you need the money? Where does that leave you? I can't fire someone for not having enough passion for what they do, especially if they do a good job. What do you think of this?"

"Well, I agree, you have to be passionate about what you do, but I think there is more than one way to do that, and there are a few ways that companies can encourage passion in their workforce. You know, my Director of Marketing here, Kelly, is a wonderful musician. She plays guitar and sings a lot and she writes songs like crazy. She's also great at marketing. So when I started making movies, I knew the best person to write the score would be Kelly. So we've created a model where she splits her time now between making music for the movies and doing her regular marketing duties.

"I like to call it 'inclusion'—we've included some of her other skill sets into her job, so she can get the maximum amount of job satisfaction. And the plus for me is I get a great Marketing Director who is happy and I get great music for my movies. Everybody wins. So that's one way that a company can increase passion and job satisfaction."

"Wow, I didn't know Kelly is a musician! The young man I was just talking to, one of my IT guys, is also a musician in a band. After talking to him he came up with the idea to DJ our corporate parties and events. He was really excited about it and I told him it's a great idea. So you would consider that an inclusion of his external skills. His musical skills have nothing to do with his job in IT, but just the fact that he gets to utilize them will increase his enthusiasm and loyalty to Bama. Hmm, I like that."

"Yes, it's really something that companies have underutilized. People are considered to be dualistic: they have their work life and their home or family life. The rest of the time they must be sleeping. It's naive to think that a person could be fulfilled by their job 100 percent of the time without any other factors being at play. We tend not to think of people as the whole, very complex organisms that they are.

"There is another way to increase someone's job satisfaction, and that is to build a culture of innovation. Innovation is naturally exciting—it's something new. Having employees get involved in the innovation company-wide, even if they're not in innovative roles, can help channel some of that creative energy that everybody has into their work.

"I've consulted with a few companies that have 'innovation hour.' Every employee, no matter their position, takes an hour three times per week, all at the same time, and just thinks. They think about what will make the company better, and what would make their lives better inside the company. Some of them think about new products, some of them think about new foods they want in the cafeteria. But putting that focus on creativity and saying to the workforce 'we think all of you have something to contribute to the well-being of this company,' that is huge. Because you are saying you trust them with the future of the organization. You are saying they are important and that they deserve to have a say. Now, you are not obligated to use any of these ideas. That's not the point. The point is that people feel bought-in to the success of the organization, and they can see their ideas being put into practice."

"Well, innovation is very important to any business. But what about when someone really does land on a great idea that could be profitable? What do you do then?"

"Well, that brings me to my next point. If that happens, and you decide to let that employee head up the project, they would take it on as if it were their own business—a business within a business. That's intra-preneurship. Intrapreneurship should be a general practice among managers and business leaders, but sadly, I don't see it very often.

"Here's a good example of intrapreneurship: A great friend of mine works for a large convenience store chain. He's in charge of shipping and receiving the trucks at all their St. Louis stores. Well, for awhile the trucks would bring all the supplies, drop them off to the stores, then they would head back to headquarters to get the next batch. On the way back, the trucks were empty. No one had thought about the potential of those empty trucks until my friend brought it up. He gave his higher-ups calculations on how much money they could be making if they picked up some extra freight jobs for the way back. His managers loved the idea, and they handed the project off to him. They told him he was in charge of the project, that he had to find the freight, negotiate the prices, talk to the drivers, everything. It was like starting and running his own trucking business, but it was within the convenience store chain. He became an intrapreneur. The business unit he runs has been very successful, and he's created it in a way that they hardly ever have to pay for freight, because the return trip pays for their own deliveries. Isn't that something?"

"So when a culture of innovation becomes fruitful, it can lead to intrapreneurship, right?"

"Yes, and that's usually how it works. Rarely would intrapreneurship ever crop up unless innovation was supported and encouraged, you know what I mean?"

"Yes, that is something. I think I told you last time that we spoke that someday I want to be a motivational speaker, like you. I just never thought it was possible, because if I were to put energy into something else, it almost felt like I was cheating on my job. But the idea that I could do that—become a speaker—and that it would actually make me better at my job, because I would be more fulfilled and confident—that's something I've never thought of."

"Well, now, you becoming a speaker is yet another kind of thing. That's what I would call extra-preneurship. Extrapreneurship is building an entrepreneurial venture outside your current scope of employment. Usually the term 'day job' comes to mind. When someone has a passion to start their own business, but doesn't have the means, then they can start small, only using their extra man hours outside of their day job. There is an increasing movement of crafters—usually women who are stay-at-home moms, or those who have jobs and do something else part-time—who sell their jewelry, art, or any number of things they've hand-crafted online. They may not make enough to cover all their bills, but the extra income helps the family and they are able to exercise their creativity. What you are talking about with your speaking career is definitely extrapreneurship. You would be responsible for the bookings and you would get paid separately from Bama. And, may I say, I think you speaking is a great idea."

"You really do? I've always wanted to do it. I speak a lot at Bama and at some local events but it's always been something I've done for free. I never thought of it as a business. I just go in and talk off-the-cuff for awhile and answer a few questions. But I have a larger message I want to get out to the world and I think speaking is a great way to do that. I will have to flex my entrepreneurial muscle and try to get the ball rolling on that. But these different forms of entrepreneurship, there's something that worries me about them. I am currently battling disengagement from my younger employees. If I tell my management team that we are going to start encouraging our employees to be more entrepreneurial, they are going to look at me like I am crazy. They will say, 'why would you want to train your workforce to quit and be self-sufficient?'"

"Yes, that is the concern that I think has prevented many companies from implementing things like this. But here is how I see it. If one of your employees has a passion to start a business, they are going to start a business eventually. It's as simple as that. But if you tie them down and say to them that they have no choice, they must work for you and single-mindedly focus on that, you are going to lose them to disengagement, or worse, they will just quit. People are people; you can't control what they love.

"Many human resources professionals would tell me I'm crazy trying to harness someone's life outside of work and use it to my own benefit, but we're not hiring robots. If someone truly loves music, they will be thinking about music while they're at work all day, whether we want to believe it or not. Either we can be supportive and gain our employees' trust by saying, 'We understand you and we trust you to still get your work done,' or we can be iron-clad and try to forbid them from being themselves.

"When you are in a job interview with someone and you ask them where they see themselves in five years, they will almost always say, 'I see myself working at this company, advancing my career,' but you and I both know that they are just saying that to get the job. If getting the job wasn't on the line they might say any number of things, and the truth is—whether they end up working for you or not, their five-year goal will still be what it was. It could be to open their own business, to have a family, to make X amount of dollars… for most people, a job is just a paycheck. But if you want to reconcile that with passion and engagement, you have to give a little freedom.

"I will always believe, though, that it's better to be a great employee than a bad entrepreneur. Not everyone is an entrepreneur and not everyone wants to be one. An old classmate of mine and I were out on our annual fishing trip, and he told me he wanted to start a business. I encouraged him and I told him that I hoped he would have the ball rolling by the next time our fishing trip came around. The next year, we went out on the boat and I asked him how the business idea was going. He looked at me and he said, 'Jim, I can't do it. I don't think I can be like you.' I was surprised and I asked him why. 'I want to see my kids' baseball games. I want to be home for dinner. I want to work and then come home and have time to relax. And I'm okay with that.'

"I had to respect him for that. You know as well as I do, Paula, that our lifestyles require sacrifices that many people do not want to make. And that's completely okay. But for people who have that extra bit of ambition, or that extra bit of energy—I think they should be given some options. Innovation, intrapreneurship and extrapreneurship are just a few ways that companies can try to harness that extra energy."

"Jim, I always get a brand new perspective when I talk to you, and you always have the best ideas. I am going to try to implement some of these ideas at Bama, and if I can't, well, I'll at least be trying to incorporate them in my own life!"

"Well, when you have an idea about this speaking thing—I mean I want you to really think about what you want to share and how you want to do it—then we can talk about it. I think you would be a great motivational speaker."

As I got off the phone with Jim, I thought about the ways I could infuse more entrepreneurial spirit into my corporation, and the benefits of doing so. Was Jim right? Would those people who were born entrepreneurs just leave eventually to follow their dreams? What about those who truly had passion for their work at Bama; how could we reward that and make sure it kept going strong? I didn't want to think of my company as a funnel with people going through and eventually coming out on the other side. My employees are not expendable. When we hire someone, we think of it as a lifelong relationship. Turnover is something we have to deal with, but I hated thinking of it as inevitable. I was sure there was something in my conversation with Jim that could help this problem. Entrepreneurship could be the answer to all of these questions.

Inclusion—Executives who have employees with talents or skills that lie outside of their regular job descriptions can try to incorporate that additional skill into the workplace. Jim's idea to have his musically-talented Marketing Director score the company's films is an excellent example.

Intrapreneurship—An employee who finds a way to incorporate a different skill or a new idea or process into existing business is an intrapreneur. This is similar to entrepreneurship, but lets a person implement their idea or plan within the boundaries of their full-time job. In a sense, it's similar to running a business within a business.

Extrapreneurship—Building an entrepreneurial venture outside your current job. The term applies to people who pursue a talent or activity for profit while maintaining their main source of employment. Extrapreneurial activities could be anything from making crafts to freelance data entry to catering events on weekends to Paula's motivational speaking.

Learning Toolkit

Entrepreneurial Takeaways

When Paula encourages Ethan to rank his passion for his job and outside interests, he acknowledges that while he enjoys his work at Bama, music is his real passion. He comes up with an idea to DJ company events, allowing him to combine his two main interests. If you are an entrepreneur at heart but work full-time for an employer, think about a way your talents might fit into the company and propose it to your manager.

Jim recognizes there is more than one way for employees to be passionate about their work, as well as for companies to encourage that passion. As an entrepreneur whose livelihood depends on the ability to fuse ideas, he knows that one person is capable of maintaining simultaneous interests, and even of combining two or more for maximum effect. He found a way for his Marketing Director to make her musical talent part of NTN, which is a win-win situation—it allows her to feel more passionate and satisfied with her job, and provides additional expertise to the company.

Entrepreneurs are natural innovators. Jim knows that encouraging employees to be innovative—whether about their own jobs or the company as a whole—is a great way to keep them thinking creatively. Most entrepreneurs rely heavily on innovation to keep their businesses growing. Take the time to think about new products or services or a new way of running your business that will keep things fresh and exciting.

If you are an employee and see an opportunity for improvement in your company, become an intrapreneur. Draw up a plan for the implementation of your idea and present it to management. You might find yourself with an interesting new second job right alongside your regular position.

Executive Takeaways

Paula gave herself the new title of Chief Culture Officer in an effort to connect with her younger staff and keep Bama's culture current and relevant to her workforce. She recognized that a strong company culture must be fostered from the top; it can't be left to chance. To understand her workers, she went right to the source and spent time with a new employee. It's important for executives to stay attuned to their employees in order to know what they need in order to be satisfied at work. Don't be afraid to ask questions and welcome suggestions; you might find that your employees have great ideas that will benefit the company.

Jim's friend, the intrapreneur, saw an opportunity that he believed would benefit his company while letting him use some additional talents. His employers were savvy enough to consider the idea seriously and put him in charge of the new project. Executives must be open to suggestions from staff; you never know where the next great idea will come from. Consider ideas that your employees bring to you and think about whether they can manage the new ideas themselves. Your employees will be encouraged and your business will benefit.

Although Paula loved her work at Bama, she harbored a dream of becoming a motivational speaker. After talking with Ethan and Jim, she realized that it's possible to do more than one job. Even the busiest executive can aspire to use other talents or follow other paths. If you have a passion other than your executive position, find a way to pursue it. The opportunity to stretch your mind will be so beneficial, both personally and professionally, because it will help you think in new and different ways.

Not everyone has the desire to be an entrepreneur—or an executive. Some employees simply do their work well and go home, yet they are valuable assets to a company. Recognition of their work ethic is just as important as recognizing the needs of the entrepreneurial employee, and good executives should be aware of both.

Chapter 11
Money is No Object

Today I sit here at the table, like I did so many years ago, only today I am not so nervous as I wait on my counterpart. Kelly reads me an article from *USA Today*—a review of my newest book, *The Ultimate Financial Plan*. I don't think I could have paid for a nicer review, and I knew we would have some time before Paula arrived. I think back to all those years ago when I waited for Paula to meet me for the first time—how different we both were—and how we have grown together, helping one another to understand the worlds in which we found ourselves.

As of today I have grown NTN to be worth millions of dollars. I have done sixteen books and five movies. I can honestly say I don't have to work for bags of groceries anymore, yet I continue my work as a business author, motivational speaker and CEO because I love what I do.

"Hi guys! So sorry about being late!" Paula arrives at our now quarterly breakfast meeting. She seems always on the run, but never out of breath. "I knew you would already be here, though, as always."

"Oh, it's no problem. How have you been, Paula?"

"Oh, things are great. I just can't wait to tell you about all that's going on."

"Well, before you do, let me ask this. It's a question I've wanted to know the answer to for awhile, and then we can catch up… how's that?"

"Okay, fire away, Jim! Your questions always get me on a new path to self-discovery." I think she was partly kidding, but I took it as a compliment anyway.

"Well, I'm working on a new project, and I want to know—why do you do what you do, if money is no longer a motivator?"

"Wow, that is a good question. Let me think about that for minute… can I tell you a little back story so I can better explain my answer?"

"I'm all ears."

"Well, some of this you know, but I'll just fill in all the gaps so you get the full picture. Last year I went down to Florida for the annual deep-sea fishing contest that McDonald's holds for their suppliers. I was on a team with a few other women, and all the other teams were all male. I cooed and cawed at the water trying to get those fish; we tried everything but we ended up coming in last. I was devastated. Not that I had ever cared about deep-sea fishing before, but getting last place… well, I guess that really lit a fire under my backside.

"I've started going down to Marathon, a small fishing town, and taking out a boat and crew every few weeks. My newest goal is to get first in that competition next year. I go down there and I meet my crew, they take me out and we catch these giant tarpon fish. I have just fallen in love with this fishing thing!

"But anyway, here is my point: those guys down there get up every morning before the sun comes up; they ride out into the water with the hope they will catch a fish. They can sell their catch at the market, but they hardly make enough to pay their bills. They fish because they love the ocean, they love fishing—they are compelled to do it. If they have a day without fishing, it's a bad day. That is how I feel about what I do. I get up every morning and I have to do this work, I have to make Bama a great place to work, I have to teach my employees that a workplace can be fun and compassionate. So to answer your question, I do it because I have to—I don't really have a choice."

"You know, that is a great way to put it. That reminds me of a story… back before I started NTN, when I still had some of my sight, I worked on the New York Stock Exchange. I did pretty well, and when you do well they reward you with these trips. They can't call them vacations, so they call them Due Diligence Trips. They were looking at investing in some property in Montego Bay, Jamaica. So they sent me down there for a couple weeks to make sure the property exists, see what kind of traffic is there, things like that. I got up early one morning and I was walking down the beach and I saw this guy collecting shells. I asked him what he was doing, and he said he swims out past where the tourists will go, collects shells and brings them back, polishes them up and sells them all day long. I asked if I could buy some of his shells and he told me, 'What I really want is those soaps you have in your hotel.' And I said, 'What for?' He told me that he could take those into town and make a lot of money.

'Where do you live?' I asked him.

'Just about 100 yards down the beach, here. What do you do?'

'I'm with the New York Stock Exchange,' I said.

'Oh, I used to be with them. I used to work my tail off fifty weeks a year so I could come down here for two. And then I realized, "What am I doing? I'm killing myself so that I can go hang out on the beach for two weeks out of the year. What's stopping me from just hanging out on the beach every day?" So I left New York and I live here full time now. If I need some money, I sell shells. If I don't feel like working, I just don't. I feel so liberated.'

"I don't know if that's the right course of action for everybody, but it worked for him. You know most of those guys on the Exchange would call him crazy, but I understand it. I would say that most people that work on the floor at Bama think to themselves, 'If I only had a tenth of the money Paula has, I wouldn't do anything at all!' That's what made me want to ask you the question."

"Well, I think it's a great question and it's the goal to be able to answer it someday, isn't it? If every business person in the world had their way, they would have the option to decide if they wanted to live on the beach and sell shells or fly around the world, or just keep on working. For me, flying around the world, getting spa treatments every day, going on retreats, buying houses—I did that for awhile. It just felt endless and meaningless. I love seeing new places, I am not complaining about my lifestyle, that's not what I mean here. I just mean that for me there is more to life than just material pleasures. I feel the most alive when I am learning new things, when I am helping people and when I am at peace with myself. None of those things requires any money at all."

"So you would say that the best ways to go from Success to Significance are through learning, helping others and finding inner peace? I think that sounds about right. For me, learning often means starting a new project that I know nothing about. It doesn't have to be a new business venture—it could be going back to school or even getting involved in an industry where you have an interest. To be honest, a lot of times learning leads me to starting another business—I mean like writing a new book or developing a new business idea with some of the organizations I serve on boards with."

"Learning a new craft, like fishing for example, makes me feel really connected, to myself and to those around me. I think as business people, sometimes everything begins to sound the same—like the teacher in Charlie Brown, wah wah wah—because we've seen it all. Quarterly statements, investment reports, all of that stuff starts to blend together. I know it's important, and of course I do my due diligence in meetings and still run my business, but I guess what I'm saying is after twenty or more years of this, it can get a little... boring. That's why learning something new can really reinvigorate your zest for life. A few years ago I took up drawing and photography. And what about you, Jim? I know you read a lot."

"I think 'a lot' may be an understatement compared to most people. I try to read one book a day, but I always have two going—one at the office and one at home. I have them in audio form, and I listen to them at five times the speed—something I've had to train my ear to do over the years. I read all kinds of books, because I am constantly looking for new material and new subjects for my columns and for future projects. But it's like you said, it's the learning that keeps me connected to that part of myself that is hungry and curious. I don't ever want to be complacent."

"That's amazing. Two books a day. I would say that I try to read one book per week, but some of them are for pleasure and entertainment. I'm really interested in ancient cultures and the 'so-called' beginning of human society. That stuff really fascinates me. But anyway, yes, I think the next big thing I would classify as helping others. There are so many things that fall under that category. I think the most obvious is philanthropy. Giving back to those causes that are really near and dear to your heart."

"Yes, I love giving back to those organizations. But one of my favorite ways to help is by sitting on advisory boards to young entrepreneurs and companies.

I really do love solving business problems, and a lot of what advisory boards do is brainstorm ways to help small, often undercapitalized companies overcome those first few years of business. Doing that work puts me right back where I was twenty years ago, but with the ability to add my experience and knowledge. I think that's invaluable to these small business owners. The kind of help that isn't monetary—that's what I think makes the biggest impact."

"You know another way I love to help is a little closer to home. My kids are getting older, and they're starting to become more business minded. My son asks business questions all the time and I love helping him understand this world. One of my daughters is getting her doctorate in psychology, so I try to learn from her how we can be a more conscious workplace, while I try to help her integrate some of the concepts from business and human resources into psychology. And my youngest daughter is actually an entrepreneur like you, Jim. That is really fun, because now they're old enough to understand why I was so busy when they were growing up and they actually want to learn from me. I think that's really cool."

"Yes, it is. Now, something that really intrigued me about what you said— inner peace. My initial reaction to that is it sounds a little ethereal, but I've been reading some things lately that indicate there's real validity to that concept. What do you mean by inner peace?"

"You know, Jim, being a business owner is not all fun and games. We have to do things that are ugly sometimes, things that we maybe don't want to do. We have to fire people, or do layoffs; we have to have hard conversations almost every day. We have to be cold and unfeeling sometimes to make the best decisions for our companies. We have to be away from our families and our kids.

"Doing all of those things, day in and day out—I think of it like dirt collecting on our souls. As an example, one of my top guys, my Chief Financial Officer, used to be a mid-level manager for Morgan Stanley. The culture there is very dog-eat-dog. Throw your employees under the bus, rat them out if they leave a few minutes early; take all the credit for all the work being done by those below you. He told me he felt sick at the end of each day because the job was turning him into the worst version of himself. To use my earlier metaphor, it was like his soul was caked in mud from years and years of buildup. He was stressed and he didn't like who he was because of the things he had to do each day. I think each of us would feel that way after awhile. Now that he's with us, he's been able to shed that mud and truly become a better person through embracing our culture and our ways of dealing with problems.

"Finding inner peace for me is a daily ritual—I can't let the dirt collect on me, so I do a daily meditation to get centered and find myself again. This term, 'inner peace'—it's not something you can find and hold, like hide and seek. It is constantly eluding us. Some people say that yoga helps, other people say that a hot bubble bath is all they need. For me I just light a candle and clear my mind for about five minutes in the morning. I've found it helps me sleep and also helps me take one thing at a time throughout the rest of the day. I think everyone should try to knock the dust off every day—we don't realize how much stuff we're carrying around until it's gone."

"That is true. The most important thing is to keep healthy, and a lot of times it's the emotional part of ourselves that we tend to forget. I really think those three principles say it all: learning, helping others and inner peace. Say, that makes me wonder—what is the most important lesson you've learned in business?"

"So many good questions today! I do have to say, and this isn't what you would expect maybe, but it's that we are all whole people. We don't have 'work selves' and 'home selves,' we can't dissect everything personal in order to put on our professional faces. Everyone is affected by every aspect of their lives—as business owners we can't ignore that people's families and relationships and health are going to affect who they are and how they perform. I think the future of business will look very different if companies and employees can embrace this truth. Companies like Google and others are figuring this out, but if you are worried about your kids or your dog then you aren't going to be able to put out your best that day. Companies large and small will become more well-rounded—day cares, fitness centers, cafeterias with healthy eating, even spas or massage therapists will become common place as people begin to integrate their personal health with their workplaces. It saves money on the bottom line too because companies with happy workers make more money. Happy employees take fewer sick days, have lower health insurance premiums and so on. I think that's the biggest lesson I've learned—and that I hope many more business owners learn. What about you, Jim, what's the biggest lesson you've learned?"

"Oh, I've been thinking about this a lot. It's sort of what we always talk about—the manager versus the entrepreneur. I have at times in my life thought that they always had to be at odds. I have realized that they don't have to be at odds, but they do have to learn to work together. I have seen so many companies fail because the owner was a great visionary who had all the earmarks of a successful entrepreneur, but when it came time to manage the business the owner was at a loss. They didn't plan for when things go wrong, and they didn't have enough money to ride it out. If they had brought on a skilled manager at the executive level, a lot of those problems could have been avoided. The opposite is true when I consult to large organizations. The executives have become comfortable and stagnant. They aren't growing, they are just managing themselves into a corner. They need innovation and entrepreneurship. My biggest lesson is learning that when these two archetypes—the executive and the entrepreneur—come together, the result is balance. Balance is something every business should strive for, and I really believe that integrating these two mindsets is the best way to get it," I said.

"I agree—I think that would be like you and me, wouldn't it?"

"Yes, I think it's exactly like you and me," I said.

"But I think, in the end, it's less about either/or. I've been an executive and an entrepreneur many times in my life—it's not the label that defines what you do. The important thing is, are you working and living with purpose? Are you making the world around you a better place?"

"Exactly. It's not about what you do, it's about how you do it. Sure, we all have strengths and weaknesses—and it's important to understand those and try to work more effectively, but the most important thing is to live passionately and let your work be reflective of that. I think that's the most important lesson I've learned in business." And as soon as I said it, I realized how true it was.

Learning Toolkit

Entrepreneurial Takeaways

When Paula tells Jim that his questions set her on a new path to self-discovery, she shows her entrepreneurial side. Asking questions and pondering the questions of others is how entrepreneurs find inspiration and solutions.

Even though Paula no longer needs to work for financial reasons, in her mind and in her heart, she still has to work. Her work—her company—is her passion. Making a difference in the lives of her employees by providing a satisfying work place is a necessity to her, not an option.

Paula feels the most alive when she is learning new things, helping people and at peace with herself. Entrepreneurs usually start out by trying to fill a void they see for a product or service, as well as their own need to make money. Once they successfully accomplish that, the drive and ambition change; money in and of itself is no longer the motivator.

Becoming complacent is a danger that successful entrepreneurs face. Once they achieve their desired goals, the main task is to stay connected to the part of themselves that is hungry and curious.

Executive Takeaways

In an odd way, the guy Jim meets who sells seashells on the beach is a good example of the traits of an executive personality. Yes, he has the obvious entrepreneurial spirit, but he made a decision based on his assessment of his goals and needs. He wanted to spend more time on the beach, so he moved there. Since he needs money, he devised a plan to generate income.

Doing due diligence is important. Having meetings, assessing how a business is doing, being aware of earnings and staying on top of things is essential to business success. These types of tasks are not necessarily exciting stuff, but thriving businesses need good executive skills to keep them that way. The executive recognizes that, and can continue to feed their personal ambitions through other learning opportunities that have nothing to do with their work.

Paula uses her daughter's insights from her psychology courses to learn how Bama can become a more conscious workplace. A good executive recognizes the need for solid employee relations and knows that business and psychology are not mutually exclusive of one another.

Being the boss—or the one in charge of making major decisions—isn't all it's cracked up to be. The hard truth is that on some days, some decisions are going to be unpopular and based on what needs to be done versus what you would want to do. Executives think with logic and level-headedness; emotions make tough decisions harder, but cannot cloud judgment if the decision is in the best interest of the company. At the end of the day, executives are human; they will feel good about some decisions, badly about others. Inner peace comes with knowing that they do the best they can with the conditions and circumstances they have to work with.

Entrepreneurial and Executive Takeaways

The value of giving back, whether financially or through mentoring, is a characteristic that entrepreneurs and executives share. Making a difference in the lives of others who want to accomplish goals is philanthropic and good business, whether by providing skills and training in a traditional office environment or by funding undercapitalized budding businesses.

Executives and entrepreneurs each have much to gain by following the three principles Jim and Paula discuss: learning, helping others and inner peace. Being open to learning new skills, hobbies or new ways of doing things; helping others to find their own passion in life or contributing to causes that touch you; and striving to achieve a level of satisfaction with who you are and how you are, take the executive and the entrepreneur from Success to Significance.

CPSIA information can be obtained
at www.ICGtesting.com
Printed in the USA
FFOW051213261212

9 781936 875085